Dear Carla —

We *all* start off as strangers.

All the best in 2022!

Cheers!

Wayne McCartney

And Then...

Networking Lessons from an Extraordinary Life Still in Progress

And Then...

Networking Lessons from an Extraordinary Life Still in Progress

Margie McCartney

And Then...
Networking Lessons
from an Extraordinary Life Still in Progress

COPYRIGHT © 2021 by
Margie McCartney

All rights reserved. Except as permitted under the U.S. Copyright Act of 1976, no part of this publication may be reproduced, distributed, or transmitted in any form or by any means, or stored in a database or retrieval system, without the prior written permission of the author.

Published by Soar 2 Success Publishing
Soar2SuccessPublishing.com

Printed in the U.S.A.
ISBN: 9781956465020

Cover photo of Margie and Gary on bicycle in front of Wrigley Field is taken by Jasmin Shah.
Photo of Chuck McCartney and Grandson on PDF page 39 and Wedding photo on PDF page 228 taken by Eric Wessman.

Table of Contents

Chapter 1	10803 - Gratitude for a Strong Start	1
Chapter 2	Camp	22
Chapter 3	Take Me Home, Country Roads	39
Chapter 4	The Lottery of Life	60
Chapter 5	It is OK to Be a BOZO!	66
Chapter 6	Planes, Trains, Automobiles, and Wrigley Field	81
Chapter 7	Making People Feel Worthy	91
Chapter 8	The Kindness of Strangers	96
Chapter 9	Dealing with A**holes	117
Chapter 10	It is a Small World After All!	122
Chapter 11	Interviews	132
Chapter 12	Golf and the People We Meet On the Course of Life	140
Chapter 13	Go With Your Gut	155
Chapter 14	One Thing Leads to Another	168
Chapter 15	When Life Gives You Lemons, Sell Them to Buy Wine!	184
Chapter 16	Be a Connector	192
Chapter 17	A Lid for Every Pot	195
Chapter 18	Making Friends Abroad	206
Chapter 19	Wanna Get Away?	214
Chapter 20	Customer Service	219
Chapter 21	Timing is Everything	235
Chapter 22	Bastogne	242
Chapter 23	The Museum of Life	251

DEDICATION

This book is dedicated to my incredibly loving
parents, Joan and Chuck McCartney

Thank you for always teaching us to
treasure people more than things.

Dad, we miss you every day.
We have kept our promise to look after Mom and she is happy.

NOTE TO READERS

This book is written to the best of my recollection. Some dates could be slightly off, and some names have been changed or omitted, and some events may have been pushed together or rearranged for narrative flow. Many important people and events in my life do not appear on these pages, because the story as written did not call for their inclusion. Maybe there will be another book in the future that will include them.

You never know… And Then… again…

ACKNOWLEDGEMENTS

Thank you to my Bethany College buddy, Allen Tait, who over thirty years ago told me, "You have to write a book one day, and when you do, you need to call it, '*And Then…*' Because, when you tell a story, it's never how you just jumped in a taxi."

"It's always, 'I jumped in a taxi… *And Then*……'"

Jimmy Clark moved from North Carolina to Chicago in 1999 and we quickly became friends, regularly playing paddle tennis at Mid-Town Racquet Club. He is a fun guy with a charming southern drawl. He was visiting my apartment one day and looked around and said to me, "Margie, I have friends that collect cars, and I have friends that collect stamps, but you collect…" And I was sure he was going to say photos, because I have a lot, but instead he said, "You collect people." I smiled and thought to myself… I guess I do.

Lucky me.

PREFACE

McCartney and Harrison Together Again

Throughout my stories, I will refer to my parents' best friends, the Harrisons. Mom met Sibby Rhodes (whom I called my "Aunt" Sibby) in seventh grade, at Pelham Junior High School, and they were loyal pals for the rest of their lives. Soon after my folks started dating at the end of 1950, they found out they both loved to play bridge. One night, they decided to each bring a friend along so they could play the game.

Mom, of course, brought her best friend, Sibby Rhodes. Sylvia by birth, she had a famous father, Phillip Rhodes. He was a naval architect known for his award-winning yacht designs. He is most well-known for designing the twelve-meter yacht, *Weatherly*, which won the America's Cup in 1963.

Dad brought his best friend and college roommate from the Phi Kappa Psi house at Cornell, Carl "Whitey" Harrison. Uncle Whitey grew up in White Plains, and his family co-founded and co-owned a heating and air conditioning company.

A second Queen of Hearts met her King that night, and then both couples were soon inseparable and fell madly in love. Two weddings followed: my parents in June 1951, and the Harrisons the following April.

The Harrisons had three children. Scott is my sister Mary's age. Doug and my brother Drew were born the same year, and Doug was often a magician at my birthday parties when I was a little girl. Diane, the baby, was born between my brother's Drew and Ray and is a creative genius. Both the sons eventually went to work for their dad's company before moving on to other careers. Diane was a product designer and buyer for high-end NYC-based retail companies. Presently, she designs gorgeous clothing and textiles in Rhode Island. My sister and I both agree that Diane has the best design taste of anyone we know. Plus, we love how she calls mom "AJ," short for Aunt Joan.

When I shared with Diane that I was writing this book, she offered to help me with the cover and I replied, "SURE!" And then… I thought, *McCartney and Harrison together again,* and smiled.

For decades, Joan and Chuck McCartney and Whitey and Sibby Harrison traveled the world together, mostly visiting various wonderful destinations in Europe. Whenever they would arrive at a hotel and say, "McCartney and Harrison checking in," the front desk clerk, nine times out of ten, said something like, "Sure you are, and where are Starr and Lennon?"

Mom is the only one left of this McCartney/Harrison foursome, but she is surrounded by photos and a lifetime of memories. And the friendship lives on through their children.

Mom, Sibby, Dad, and Whitey enjoying a day on the water.

"If in a day, you can make someone happy,
And make yourself happy, too—
Then you can say this day has meant something and,
Can ask no more of it."

M. Simmons
Warwick, Rhode Island

The God Squad: Margaret Sisto, Mom, Father Ernest Frimpong and Cacky Gregware in front of OLPH Church in Pelham Manor, NY. My grandfather, John Ray Maust, donated the bells in the background to the church in the 1960s.

Chapter One

10803
Gratitude for a Strong Start

Most people never forget their first pet, their first friend, their first kiss, or their first zip code.

10803 is the zip code for Pelham, New York. Located just thirty minutes from the Big Apple, Pelham was an ideal place to grow up. I never realized when I was young how lucky I was to live there. I just assumed that my awesome childhood was how pretty much everyone else lived their lives too. Later in life, I met many folks from around the world and soon realized how fortunate I was. Pelham was very green, almost like a big park. I can vividly remember driving home from many road trips with my family seeing the canopy of large, leafy trees through the car window, and knowing we were almost home. Pelham is near the north shore of the Long Island Sound in Westchester County, fifteen to twenty minutes from both Greenwich, Connecticut and the George Washington Bridge, and eight minutes from City Island, in the Bronx. A special town with great restaurants, art centers, libraries, and shops, both I-95 and the Hutchinson River Parkway go thru Pelham, so it is easy to get around. For the traveling McCartney clan, it's always been convenient that Pelham is also only twenty minutes to LaGuardia Airport, over the Whitestone Bridge. On any given day there are probably a few of us in the sky.

It was an easy commute for my father into Grand Central Station each morning on the Metro North train. Pelham has many beautiful homes and sidewalks too. Fortunately, we could walk to school.

We had four elementary schools that fed into Pelham Junior High (seventh and eighth grade) and then Pelham Memorial High School (PMHS). I went to Prospect Hill where my mother had gone and my four siblings before me. Mom could drive us around Pelham and tell us, almost house for house, who lived there over the years, as she has spent all but two of her ninety-two years on this earth in Pelham. Not only did she know most of the parents, but she could tell you the names of their kids and what sports they played, and what they were doing now. I always felt like Mom was an honorary mayor of Pelham. You could offer to buy her a house anywhere in the world and she would say, "No thanks, I'd rather live in Pelham!"

We walked home for lunch every day from Prospect Hill Elementary School. Mr. Chris was a janitor at Prospect Hill and a friendly, kind soul. One brisk morning, I woke up early. No one was home except my grandmother, who lived with us at the time. I must have been in kindergarten because I could not read the clock in the kitchen. Unbeknownst to me, they had all gone to church on Wednesday, for the start of Lent. I was sure I was late for school, so I ran all the way to Prospect Hill (maybe six zig-zaggy blocks), afraid I would get in trouble. Mr. Chris was mopping the floor and said to me, "School doesn't start for another hour!" and I raced back home. They were all back from church by then and I remember that Mom made me hot cocoa with little marshmallows in it and then later drove me back to Prospect Hill. But my eagerness to get to school wasn't just on schooldays; I also, admittedly, used to run from my bed to the top of the banister on Saturday mornings yelling, "Mom, I am late for school!" and she would yell upstairs, "It's Saturday, you can go back to bed." I was a social animal even then. Never wanted to miss a thing.

Getting to school was also important because when I was five, I met my life-long friend, Heather McLeod. I cannot remember if they sat us alphabetically in kindergarten, but somehow these two Mc's met and from that moment on, we were thick as thieves. We did everything together from playing with the dollhouse that my brother, John, and Dad made me for Christmas, to being active athletes. She was on the tennis team, and I played on the softball and volleyball squads. The two of us were also cheerleaders together at PMHS.

Many of our favorite memories revolved around weekend ski trips to Vermont. Our neighbors on Bon Mar Road, the Lightfoots, had a house near Bromley Mountain in Vermont, and we would go up with their family. It was always so much fun, and we really came alive in that spectacular setting. There is nothing like the beauty of freshly fallen snow and the thrill of heading down a mountain on skis with a song in your heart. That first chairlift ride in the morning is so still and calm; you can hear your heartbeat. To watch the sun breaking through the trees onto the snow is magic.

My parents eventually bought a small house called "Spot in the

Sun" in Peru, Vermont. Many a weekend or vacation was spent in Vermont in those years. Our house was set off the main road, and we knew to put our left blinker on when we saw a sign that read, "Pigeons and Firewood" across the road. Dad used to love to drive into the small town of Peru and chat with all the locals. Surrounded by woods, my siblings and I would race snowmobiles around the back roads and compare times between our teams of two. After skiing all day, I would relish in the joy of taking our long-haired black Labrador, Sugar, on long walks through the forest, jumping from rock to rock through the creeks. We got our sweet Sugar at the local pound. She loved everyone and way before there were leash laws, would follow strangers home to neighboring towns and they would call us. I can only imagine how much money Dad spent tipping people for calling us to come get our wandering dog!

Several years ago, my mom, my sister Mary, and I went up to Manchester, Vermont to stay at the Equinox Resort for Easter, taking a trip down memory lane. Most homes in the area, like the Equinox Inn, are painted white with either green or black shutters. That architectural look goes on for miles in every direction. Quintessential New England for sure! We drove by the very first house we rented long ago, then past the old Jelly Mill, which now sells clothes. Later, while leaving town, we drove by our old little "Spot in the Sun" in Peru. It is now a garage for a very large house! It served its purpose for us and gave us many wonderful memories that I will always treasure.

One memory was when we were probably in junior high school, Heather was up with us in Vermont and my parents went out for dinner. The toilet overflowed and we did not know what to do. I

And Then...

called my brother Drew in New York but he had no suggestions. Heather had an idea: "Let's vacuum up the water!" I thought it was a great idea and secretly wished I had thought of it first. We got my mom's old round yellow Hoover vacuum out of storage and took it down to the bathroom. We plugged it in and put the attachment right into the toilet, got all the water out, and put it away. We never told anyone. We even took our socks and shoes off so they would not get wet, and we would not have to tell my parents what had happened.

A few weeks later when we were in Vermont again, Mom asked me to go get the vacuum. While carrying it down the stairs, it started to drip on my pants, so I felt like I had to come clean. Mom went *crazy* telling me how stupid we were. We could have been electrocuted. At the time, we were so proud that we got up all the water! Sometimes it is hard to learn a lesson when, in your eyes, you are doing something right.

Clearly, this was a lesson I never really grasped. On a previous occasion, while still in elementary school, Mom had told me to take a bath before dinner, but I wanted to watch *I Love Lucy*. I figured I could try to do both simultaneously. I pushed the TV as far down the hall as it would go into the bathroom, but still could not see the screen. So, I plugged the earpieces into the TV and put the buds into my ears so I could take a bath *and* listen to Lucille Ball, my childhood idol. Suddenly, I heard a scream as my mom yanked the earplugs from my ears, yelling at me. I think it was the episode where Harpo Marx played "Take Me Out to the Ballgame" on the harp after the Ricardos and Mertzes had moved to California. This was not only one of my favorite episodes, but many years later, I would hire a harpist for my own wedding to play "Take Me Out to the Ballgame" as we walked back down the aisle after our marriage ceremony! Oh, how I loved Lucy!

But these close shaves have Heather and I agreeing that we must have a purpose in life to still be alive! There are more stories, but I will leave it at that.

In her late twenties, Heather married a great guy named Jamie Greacen, whom I adore. I had the privilege of being their maid of honor. As the years ensued, they had two children: Kelly, born on my birthday, June 8th, and Scott, named after Heather's brother who had died in 1985. It was a gift to be asked to be a Godmother to them both.

I always thought I would have children of my own, but I am blessed to have two nieces, Madeleine and Lauren, and four nephews: Charlie, Sam, Liam, and Evan. It is truly a gift to be an aunt! Additionally, I am grateful for my five Godchildren.

When I was in high school, my mom was teaching fourth grade at Hutchinson Elementary School with her buddy Rocco Polera, who was the principal at the time. Rocco was also the Director of Instrumental Music for the Pelham Public School District, and a very well-respected man throughout Pelham. Apparently, a teacher had gone on a two-year sabbatical at "Hutch," and Rocco knew my mom had a teaching degree, so he asked her to fill in. Though she had her degree, I do not think she ever really thought she would use it, but she did, and we were all very proud of her.

Years later, after I moved to Chicago, I went to Des Moines, Iowa

And Then...

on a sales trip and took in a minor league Cubs game where Gary Scott was playing third base for the Iowa Cubs, the farm team for the Chicago Cubs. He was from Pelham and my mom had been his fourth-grade teacher at Hutch. I passed a note through a groundskeeper to him in the dugout, and he met me outside the Cubs locker room after the game. I scurried to the parking lot post-game, and as he was walking out of the locker room door, he saw me and said, "Your mom was really tough!"

I said, "You don't need to tell me that. I am her daughter; I know!" In retrospect, I am so grateful she was.

Mom insisted that we write thank you notes. When I was young, I would roll my eyes when she told me to do that. Now, I understand that it is one of the most valuable lessons she passed on. She would say, "You only need to write a few sentences. People just want to know you appreciate what they did, said, or how they made you feel."

Over the years, many of Mom's friends have told me that she is the most loyal friend you could ever have. I remember at Aunt Sibby's funeral, Diane Harrison said, "Joan McCartney is a fiercely loyal friend." Not just loyal, but *fiercely loyal*. I loved that and it is so true. There is really no one better to have on your side. One Christmas, my sister Mary gave us all T-shirts with sayings on them. Mom's said, "Tough but Fair." Perfect.

When Mary got to high school, she saw our older brother John in the hall and said, "Hello." John said to her, "Don't say hello to me. Don't tell anyone you know me!" Classic upperclassmen treatment of freshmen. Mary told Mom, and Mom made John walk

Mary to school every day. Mom followed behind them in her car going 5 mph to make sure he did not ditch her. Ironically, my brother Drew did the same thing to me. I do not remember if he got the same punishment. However, later that year, he got a different punishment that was probably worse. Imagine being an all-county middle linebacker on the football team your senior year, getting ready to go play ball at the University of Virginia, and having your homeroom teacher announce in class that your mother had called, and you had to go home because you did not make your bed!

At PMHS, there was a math teacher named Ms. Holt. One day, my mom ran into Ms. Holt at the grocery store at the check-out counter. Ms. Holt said, "Hi, Joan, we certainly hope that Drew's mononucleosis is better; we sure have missed him in math class the past few weeks." Mom looked at her and replied, "He is much better. You will see him tomorrow." She never ratted him out to his teacher but went home and handled it in her own special way. Drew was in class the next day.

Mom laughed when other Pelham moms bragged that their kids were *so* perfect. She was too smart to ever say that about the five of us. Although I know she loves to brag about us, she always felt the moment you said something like, "My child is perfect," they would be caught stealing candy at the five and dime. No kid (or no one really) is perfect.

One summer, Drew was a busboy at a high-end private club. He got fired by a guy he felt had it out for him all along, for eating a steak that had been mistakenly ordered for a customer and he had been told to enjoy. He told Mom what had happened. Drew recalled the story at Mom's 85th birthday party (through tears of pride). That day, she jumped into her woody station wagon and drove down to the club. She said to the man, "My son is not perfect, but he is not a thief" and asked him to give my brother his job back. He said, "NO!" We heard that this man was fired soon afterward. No tears were shed in our house!

Mom had quite the Pelham network, and we would always get found out for doing something we were not supposed to do. Mrs. Henningsen seemed to always see Drew out someplace that my mom had told him *not* to go to. Later, she would casually mention it to Mom. There seemed to be no secrets in Pelham.

Just days before my parents and the Harrisons were leaving on vacation for Europe in 1979, my friend Polly McGwire and I got caught in the hall at PMHS a minute or two after the bell rang for class. The hall monitor dragged us down to the principal's office and treated us rudely. We could not believe it. I went home after school, feeling battered, and told Mom what had happened, and she was very upset. Not at *me*, but at the hall monitor who treated us cruelly. (Again, I am *certainly* not perfect, but it is not like we were smoking or drinking in the hall; we had the next period off, and we were going to get lunch.)

That night, while I was falling asleep in bed across the hall from my parents' bedroom, I heard my mom on the phone with Bobbie McQueen, who was on the Pelham Board of Education. I was friends with Mrs. McQueen's daughters, Cathy and Lori, at PMHS. Cathy and I played softball together, and Lori taught me to sink a basketball while standing under the net, onehanded, using the backboard. That skill helped me be competitive playing HORSE with my nieces and nephews for years to come. Mom said that PMHS should be grateful to have the group of girls we hung out with representing Pelham in so many ways. I fell asleep crying that night, so grateful that I had a mom who would stand up for me and my friends!

When I was seventeen and a senior, my parents went to a USA vs. Russia hockey game at Madison Square Garden in NYC. It was the end of the school year, and we were coasting by at that point, as we all pretty much knew where we were going to college. It seemed like every Thursday night; someone would have a party. Since my folks were going into the city that night to the hockey game, I told my friends that we could have a party at our house. (Very dumb, but seemingly brilliant at the time!) At the end of the second period of the hockey game, I shared that everyone should probably leave because my parents were known for leaving sporting events early to beat the traffic. (We had firsthand experience with this. Much to our dismay, we often ended up missing the end of a Giants game and had to listen to the fourth quarter on the car radio on the way home to beat the traffic!) Everyone at the party was having so much fun, they wanted to stay. I was in a festive mood and thought, what the hell…

So, while I was sitting by the fireplace with a Groucho Marx nose and glasses on, and a Budweiser in my hand, Heather and Amy Corbett came running up from downstairs where the garage was and shouted, "Margie, your parents are home!" There must have been twenty cars out front, and suddenly, here comes Mom in her mink coat and Dad following her into the room. You've never seen so many people take off from a party so fast in your life. Someone took a tablecloth and wrapped up all the beer cans,

And Then...

ashtrays, etc. from a table and ran out the door with it. My friends were all politely saying, "Hello, Mrs. McCartney. Goodbye, Mrs. McCartney. Hello, Mr. McCartney, Goodbye, Mr. McCartney." And out they went. Mom stood there yelling at me, which I expected, but my dad just said, "I am so disappointed in you," which cut like a knife.

The next morning, I woke up very early. I was wary of more yelling and disappointment, but also, Heather and I had a lead role in one of the skits for the Sr. Class Talent Show both Friday and Saturday nights. Plus, two of my camp friends (Tom Hopkins, a.k.a. Hopper, and Phil Garvey) were coming in from Brooklyn and Long Island, so I was in a great mood. I did not want to start the day off on a bad note. I walked up to Heather's house across from Prospect Hill at around 5:30 a.m. Knowing that her family never locked their door, I snuck in and slept on her pink and green flowered couch in their den. Her dad came down in his boxers to get the morning paper and went to wake Heather and give her the daily weather report, as he did every morning. He noticed me on the sofa, and we said hello. He woke Heather up and said, "It's going to be a nice warm day, and Margie is on the couch downstairs." She came running down the stairs, surprised to see me. I told her I had to get out of my parents' house before another round of reprimands came.

The good news was that the play went great. My parents were there and loved it. The next day, when I went down to the kitchen for breakfast, Mom said "Don't think I am not mad about Thursday night, but you were great in the play." Phew! Thank God for that play!

10803 Gratitude for a Strong Start

For the first sixteen years of my life, we lived in a big, beautiful, light-pink, Spanish house with a red-tiled roof on Bon Mar Road in Pelham Manor. We moved to Bon Mar Road from half a mile away when I was not even a year old. We had a great lady who lived with us named Maria Romero. Maria had been living with and working for a family who decided to move back to South America. Maria did not want to return to Chile, though; she wanted to stay in Pelham. Every time she turned around, my mom was having another baby. Maria figured her neighbor might need some help with five kids. One day, Maria knocked on Mom's kitchen door and said, "Is it okay if I work for you?" She moved in the next day. I was a newborn and Maria did not move back to Chile until I graduated from college. She wrote and told us she had named her new dog in Chile, Ray, after my brother. I think he was her favorite. Ray typically caused the least amount of trouble. Maria was amazing and helped Mom out with all of us, coming and going in a million directions with sports and activities. She also cooked a mean chicken and rice dinner!

I'm not exactly sure where the cow bell came from that my folks used to ring on Bon Mar Road to call us in for dinner, but it was loud, and we knew it was for us. Anyone on the block knew Mom's cow bell. Even if I somehow missed it, someone else would say, "Margie, it's time for you to go home for dinner." Typically, my family all sat together at dinnertime. We would wait till the boys got home from football or basketball or wresting practice and Dad got home from the train station. We would tell stories of our day and sneak food to our dog under the table. We always had pets.

Bon Mar Road is a very special and unusual street. It is shaped

And Then...

like a half moon or a big smile. Our house was in the middle of the larger curve or lower lip. There was and still is a big island in the middle of the street. My neighborhood friends and I could play in several treehouses, climb trees, and play house, raking leaves into imaginary rooms. We had five kids in our family, and that was typical for the families on our block. On Friday nights, many Bon Mar-ites met in our backyard to play Kick the Can or SPUD or hide-and-go-seek, easily twenty or more of us on a regular basis. We always felt safe, and we always looked after each other. I fondly remember all my former stellar neighbors. It was a delightful childhood!

Mom always showed up on the doorstep of someone new on the block with a casserole. Forever Friendships were born. Rita and Judd Vear moved to our street from Chicago when I was five. Rita Vear was one of Mom's best friends till she died about ten years ago and my dad and Judd were great pals as well. Another family, the Strianos, moved from Rome to Bon Mar Road around the same time. Mom and I re-connected with Nikki Striano in Rome a few years back. It was like no time had passed when they were together.

When I was two, our next-door neighbors on Bon Mar Road had a baby girl named Sallie Saunders. Sallie was bald for years, and her mom used to tape a pink bow on her head so people would know she was a girl. Sallie and I spent countless hours as toddlers playing in the muddy pachysandra that covered both of our front yards. (No grass to mow!) We made mud cakes and were as happy as could be. We would always be at each other's birthday parties and years later, she and her husband, John Colucci, from Queens bought our old house on Bon Mar Road. They raised their three awesome children in that house and eventually hosted my wedding in her (my old) backyard! Our ceremony was by the dogwood tree we always used for home plate when we played wiffleball or kickball as kids. I loved telling people I got married at "home plate."

Sallie was my very first friend and all these years later, it still feels like she is my sister from another mother. Her mom, Merrie Gayle Schmidt Saunders, was from New Orleans and grew up in a large house on St. Charles Avenue. The trolleys run up and down St. Charles Avenue, and it is a main thoroughfare in that great city. Several years ago, my friend and former colleague, Jeff O'Hara, told me that he and his team organized a huge industry party for 450 people for Starwood hotels in the house Merrie Gayle Saunders grew up in. It is called *The Brown Mansion*. In a city known for its grand homes, in the opinion of many, Mrs. Saunders home was the grandest home on the grandest avenue. Unfortunately, that house was sold long ago, so when Mrs. Saunders died, all that was left for Sallie to inherit was some swamp land.

We were lucky that our parents came to almost all our sporting events. All three of my brothers played football, and Mom used to bring that famous cow bell that would ring over the hillside announcing her and Dad's arrival at any away games. One of the football announcers at Parkway Field for the home games, Mr. Sanders, was a fan of my parents. Mom was always involved with the PTA, and Dad was President of the Booster Club in Pelham that helped support Pelham Athletics. So, whenever there was a question about who made a tackle, if it wasn't obvious, Mr. Sanders would just say into the mic, "Tackle by McCartney." The cow bell would ring again.

And Then...

I was a cheerleader and loved every minute of it. I was honored to be elected Captain as a senior, along with Amy Corbett. We had so much fun cheering for our friends, going with the football team for breakfast before the games at the Colonial Diner, practicing, and learning new cheers. We competed and *won* a competition in White Plains once at the Civic Arena, which was a big thrill. We had some great, cute, fun, unique cheers, and one of my favorites was: "Got the Spirit, you know it; Got the Spirit, Gonna show it." I would practice this *full energy* in the living room, much to my brothers' dismay. Since all three of my brothers played football, I had some advanced knowledge of the sport; I had started watching the two of them play in the local Youth Football Pop Warner league. Our squad knew I would typically start the cheer for *offense* or *defense*!

The home football games at PMHS on Saturdays at Parkway Field will be on my highlight reel of life that they say flashes before your eyes before you die. Standing pre-game on the field while they played the National Anthem, elbows bent with blue and white pom poms… I get chills just remembering it! Marching in the Thanksgiving Day Parade in New Rochelle (the next town over) in our new Pelham Memorial High School cheerleading uniforms was a thrill too. We went door to door selling greeting cards to raise money for those new uniforms and felt quite spiffy!

We all had a great sense of Pelham pride while representing our town. Our mascot was the Pelicans. When I got to college, people would laugh when they saw my sweatshirt with "Pelham Pelicans" on it and a picture of the bird with the huge beak. However, I joined the charge to keep that mascot when, while at PMHS, someone was trying to change it to the Pelham Patriots. There are many schools with a Patriot mascot, but we were unique being the Pelicans!

I remember once getting a humorous birthday card with a Pelican on the front that read, "What can a doctor do that a Pelican can't?" Then you opened the card and it said, "Stick its bill up its ass!"

In March of 1979, our senior year at PMHS, my friends and I decided to cut school and head into NYC for the St. Patrick's Day parade. We all met up at the Pelham Train Station for the thirty-minute ride into Grand Central Terminal. It was fun to be doing something different, and we were having a great day wearing green gear and cheering for all the bands and Irish dancers. It was also fun doing something we were not supposed to be doing! We all had a blast but were a little bit nervous the next day. Apparently, daily, the school administration would type up and distribute to all the faculty a list of students who had not been in school on any given day. On March 18th, our friend, Carolyn Capo's, aunt (who was a Phys Ed teacher) dropped off the absentee list from March 17th at her mom's house and left it on the dining room table with our names circled in bright *red*!

We realized we should have thought about that attendance list.

My mom's favorite holiday has always been Memorial Day. I remember once in May of 2006; Mom and I went up to Cooperstown and stayed at the Otesaga Resort Hotel and visited

And Then...

the Baseball Hall of Fame. (A trip I would duplicate on my honeymoon!) Mom was seventy-six at the time and had stopped golfing, but I had a free round of golf at the Leatherstocking Golf Course at Otesaga and asked Mom to play at least nine holes with me. It came as no surprise when she parred the first par three hole! I called my brother Drew to brag about her, and he said we could take her on the road. "Ladies and Gentlemen, step right up, watch the lady shoot her age!"

She had said she wanted to make sure we were back to Pelham for the Memorial Day Parade. On Monday morning, we went to 8 a.m. Mass at OLPH (Our Lady of Perpetual Help) Church, and there were maybe thirty people in attendance. There was a visiting priest who did not speak English well, and he did not mention that it was Memorial Day. Suddenly, as the Mass was ending, I saw Mom marching up the aisle to the altar and I thought to myself, *What is she going to do now?* She stopped on the altar, turned to face the Congregation, and said, "Today is Memorial Day and I think it would be nice if everyone said a prayer for our troops." She got a standing ovation and I cried, so proud of my mom for having the courage to do what others would not. That was how she rolled.

During the Pelham Memorial Day parade when we were little, my brother Ray and my friends and I would attach cards to our bicycle spokes with clothespins and ride around the parade route. We just loved the sound those cards made, and it was such a festival. Thousands of people lined the streets in red, white, and blue, and the parade went from one side of town all the way to the other. Mom and her best friend, Aunt Sibby, would stand with their flags on the Esplanade, just off Black Street while the parade went by. They both knew *all the words* to the Pelham High fight song seventy years later and would stand and sing it while the PMHS band marched by! AH-MAZE-ING!

Sports has always been a big background in my family's life. We spent Sundays either at Yankee Stadium or Shea Stadium watching football when I was a little girl. We attended weekly Mass at OLPH Church in Pelham and loved when Father Skelly said Mass, particularly during football season because he talked very fast and said: "Inthenameofthefatherandofthesonandoftheholyspirit Massisendedgoinpeace" like it was one word. We secretly thought he was sneaking out the back door of church to grab deli sandwiches at Remi's Deli (the best!) on Boston Post Road and head to tailgate pre-game too! My sister, Mary, bleeds Jet Green but my brothers and I are Giants Fans all the way! Go Blue!

In 1999, my dad was the Grand Marshal of the Pelham Memorial Day parade, which was a big thrill for all of us. I had run into Bob McGuirl, a Pelham resident who served two tours in Vietnam and had a lifelong devotion to veteran's causes as a volunteer and leader and a member of the American Legion. He also ran the Pelham Memorial Day parade, and he told me that he had asked my dad to be the Grand Marshal of the parade, and that my dad had said no. I was shocked but should have realized my father's humility. I confronted my dad and he asked, "Is it important to you?" I said, "Yes, it's important to me and everyone who loves you. You deserve this. You are a hero." My dad fought in Patton's 3rd Army in the Battle of the Bulge in WWII and earned a bronze

And Then...

star and two purple hearts. He never talked about the war 'til decades later. The day he was the Grand Marshal, we hosted a party in our backyard in Pelham, and most of the town and our friends and some relatives came. Many wonderful speeches were given in front of the town hall, and we were all as proud as peacocks. Even friends from Dublin, Ireland came. Everyone said repeatedly how thrilled they were to be a part of something so special. Dad was always our hero, but it was nice to share our hero with the rest of Pelham and friends from around the world.

The day of the parade, Dad had my nephew, Sam (who was about three years old at the time) on his lap in a red convertible while he gave the queens' wave with that big Irish grin to everyone along the parade route. Interesting to note that two of my nephews became US Marines, following in both of their grandfathers' footsteps to serve. Another hero, their maternal grandfather served in the US Navy on a ship during the Korean War.

I'm so grateful that Mom, Mary, and I got to take Dad to the WWII Memorial dedication in Washington DC in May 2004. Dad had trouble walking at that point from multiple war wounds. He had to have many of the veins in his legs rerouted through surgery at one point. We had a little seat carrier that Dad could rest on when we had a long way to walk, usually for a football game when we had to park far away. But even before his walking deteriorated, Dad never was one to exercise much. He liked to play golf and paddle tennis, but that was about it. He would rather take a cab to the men's room than walk, often saying, "I walked across Europe during the *war*!" We would reply "Yes, Dad but then you walked to defeat Hitler. Now we want you to walk for *you*!"

But he did play his role in defeating Hitler, so while in DC for the dedication, my dad was wearing his medals pinned to his suit. It was dusk as we were walking from the WWII Memorial, when a young man, maybe fifteen years old, sort of pushed through the crowd to approach my dad. I was not sure what his intentions were, and felt like SWAT, quickly putting myself between the stranger and my father. Then, the young man extended his hand to my dad and said, "I just want to say, thank you for your service, sir."

A year later, Dad died.

And Then...
I was reminded how important it is to do things *now* and not wait for the next opportunity. *Today* may be the only chance you have!

It's recently become abundantly clear to the world that tomorrow is promised to no one. If you knew you only had a short time left, what would you do differently? Why not do that now?

Is there someone you have not spoken to in a long time that you want to catch up with? Is there a place you want to visit or return to? What is holding you back?

I'll challenge you to GO FOR IT NOW—don't wait another day to reconnect with past friends, teachers, even family members. It's never too late to have a conversation.

And Then...

Dad as the Grand Marshal of the Pelham Memorial Day parade in 1999 with his grandson, Sam, on his lap. Sam and his brother Charlie both grew up to become U. S. Marines.
Photo taken by Eric Wessman.

Camp

Chapel at Our Lady of Lourdes Camp on Forest Lake in Livingston Manor, NY (1976).

The Red Team, Summer '77.

Chapter Two

Camp

In the summertime, from probably the age of five to ten, I went to Badger Day Sports Camp in Larchmont, New York. I loved going to camp and I loved Badger. We had swim meets, played sports and games, and sang songs. It was competitive and fun. I was on Bus #2 and Joan was our counselor. It's funny, the things you remember! Badger was not a sleep-away camp, but it laid the foundation for the fun that was yet to come.

The next June, I turned ten and went to a two-week Girl Scout camp in Mountain Lakes, New Jersey right after school ended. When my mom picked me up on the last day, I was expecting to go to a horseback-riding camp a few days later in Pennsylvania, called Tegawitha. My sister Mary had gone there and loved riding horses. However, Mom said she changed her mind at the last minute when her sister told her about a Catholic sports camp called Our Lady of Lourdes Camp for Girls in the Catskill Mountains. My aunt had gone there and loved it. I was like, "What? Church camp?! I don't want to go to Church Camp!!!???!!!???!!!??"

My life changed forever, *for the better.*

Our Lady of Lourdes Camp for Girls (OLL) opened in Livingston Manor, NY on June 2, 1920, on Forest Lake. The land next to OLL

Camp was purchased by Camp Acadia for Boys, (OLL's brother camp) and opened on Lake Uncas on June 29, 1923. Lake Uncas is only 500 yards from Forest Lake as the crow flies, but the road winds around so the walk is longer, more like a mile. The boys' camp had originally been in Lake Ronkonkoma on Long Island since 1908, until they purchased 505 acres upstate near OLL. Little did those men leading teams of oxen to clear the land for a boat house, chapel, tent colony, pavilion, and mess hall know at the time, but they were literally laying the groundwork for years of happiness for over 200 children every summer. The camp boundaries were marked by piles of stones. We probably passed them on hikes to Beaverkill through the woods, without even knowing! I never knew the actual boundaries; it was just miles of woods to me, and I loved when we would blaze new trails, figuring out a shortcut over the mountains.

At both the boys' and girls' camps, there were age brackets and accompanying names. The youngest campers were Minims, ages five to seven. Juniors were eight to nine and then came the Intermediates, who were ten and eleven years old. Next up came the Sub Seniors, who were twelve and thirteen, and the Seniors were fourteen, fifteen, sixteen, and seventeen years old. However, you could also become a Counselor in Training (CIT) at seventeen, which I did. Then I went on to be the Sub Senior Division Leader supervising forty-six twelve and thirteen-year-old girls the next summer. Talk about a challenge, but so much fun too! Eventually, in the summer of 1982, my last summer at OLL, I became the Athletic Director.

If I remember correctly, we had Mass every Sunday, in addition to all camp Mass once a week and divisional Mass once a week and

And Then...

Benediction on Sunday. I do remember writing my mom once saying that I was pretty much covered for Mass until I was sixty!

My first summer at Our Lady of Lourdes Camp was the summer of '72 and I was an Intermediate. One of my favorite counselors that summer was named Marjorie Loperfido. My birth name is Marjorie and I had not met another Marjorie besides my name's sake: Marjorie Burns Weihman.

The Head Counselor of the girls' camp was named Anne McGrath. She and her husband Doc Terry met as teenagers at camp, and they lived in Chappaqua, NY. Doc was a dentist, and he would drive up on the weekends and was usually busy organizing whatever project needed fixing that day. Mrs. McGrath, like my mother Joan McCartney, was tough but fair. Just recently on our camp Facebook page, I posted an old photo of the counselor staff from 1978, and two gals commented, "I remember all fondly, especially Mrs. McGrath. She reminded me of my mother who had passed a few years before I started at OLL." Another camper wrote, "Mrs. McGrath was so nice; she ran OLL like a well-oiled machine, all the while making sure each camper had a happy and healthy time at camp."

Color War was *huge* at camp. There were two teams, the Red and the Orange, and they fought like their lives depended on it throughout the summer in every sport there is, plus swim meets and track meets. A lot was riding on winning Color War, mainly pride, but there were also other perks. For example, on banquet night, the winning team got to eat steak and potatoes and eclairs, while the losing team had to sit on the floor of the mess hall and eat hash. With the good and the bad, Color War

Camp was just SO. MUCH. FUN!

Since my Aunt Sally had been on the Red Team, I was happy when on the night in the Pavilion when teams were chosen, I was picked to be on the Red Team. At the boys' camp, they had you switch teams each month. I guess they figured boys were competitive enough that they did not need a lifelong membership to Red or Orange.

The McGraths had four daughters—Sally, Kathy, Mary, and Maureen—who all attended camp. Each of them wonderful people and great athletes. Sally, the oldest, was on the Red Team, but Kathy, Mary, and Maureen were all on the Orange Team. My counselor, Marjorie, had a younger sister Marilyn Loperfido who was Red Team Captain my first summer at camp. Her co-captain was a Pelham girl named Sue. I always thought Marilyn was very cool and fun and Sue was an awesome athlete. Sue could hit a softball from home plate on the baseball field, across the hockey field and into the woods. I saw her do it and my jaw dropped open. I loved being a part of everything at camp. It was all new and exciting, and I was very happy with all the activities. This was for sure a better fit than just horseback-riding camp for me. Plus, OLL did have stables and we could ride horses there too, but there was so much more! And I think that my love for Birch trees was born at camp, riding horses through paths in the fields and woods that were surrounded by Birch trees. I loved not only the sound of the wind blowing through the trees, but how the leaves on the trees would shimmer in the sunlight and look like silver dollars. I can close my eyes and be back there right now. I can even remember the smell of horse dung, but it was all part of the experience. Sasha was my favorite horse, and she was black with a white star on her nose.

The youngest McGrath daughter, Maureen (nicknamed Mooie because her sister Mary could not pronounce Maureen), was an Intermediate with me my first year. I was not thrilled with my tentmates initially, and Mooie became my best pal quickly and has remained so to this day. From the moment I arrived at camp, she was always nice, friendly, and welcoming. Though a small fry, she was an outstanding athlete. Sometimes, I would crash in her tent sleeping head to toe in her cot. She had been there the summer before and knew the ropes. We have always made a good duo, and to this day, I always say that I make sure Mooie has fun, and she makes sure I do not go to jail! Camp friends are forever friends.

But Mooie was on the Orange Team, so it seemed we were always competing against each other, whether it was running in a track meet or swimming or rowing at the waterfront. In all our years of amazing friendship, I think the only fight we had was about a charades game in the mess hall when we were about sixteen. During the Summer of 1977, I was Red Team Captain. Being Captain of the Red Team was a *huge honor* for me. It is certainly one of my proudest accomplishments in life that the Red Team won Color War in both July and August that summer.

There were a *ton* of team songs, and we sang them all the time, which was wonderful. These songs were part of the camp tradition and were passed down through the years. For example, at the beginning of each sporting match, we would sing "Dedicated to this Game" and each team would sing a song for their color. At the end of every sporting match, whether soccer, or speed-away

Camp

(a great game that combines basketball, soccer, and football, which I *loved*!) or the Apache Relay, which kicked off Color War, we always sang "Pals, Dear Old Pals."

There were so many highlights from camp that it is hard to remember them all… The Apache Relay started off Color War, and at the girls' camp it was set up to portray a typical day at OLL. It started with a Minim or Junior getting out of a bed (in her bathing suit) and getting dressed by a cot that was set up on the Junior ballfield. Then she would pass a baton to someone who would wrap the tetherball ball around the pole, then someone would eat three crackers and whistle a tune, followed by two gals hitting a badminton shuttlecock over the net five times. Then someone would sink three pointers on the basketball courts, do a tennis volley up to five times, kick a soccer ball back and forth across the length of the soccer field, then dribble a hockey ball with a field hockey stick back and forth, then throw a softball back and forth. Someone would run the road to bug island and then canoe back to the girls' float, swim to the dock, race up the hill, and hand the baton to someone who would get back into bed to end the race. It was thrilling every time with over 100 girls *screaming* for their teams, their voices simultaneously echoing over the mountains.

We had wonderful canoe trips down the Delaware River, where we would pull over and swim and use rope swings off trees and eat our sandwiches for lunch. So many late-night conversations about *everything* with your tentmates, learning how to use tampons, sneaking over to the boys' camp, summer romances, KP/Busboy trips to Grossingers, Varsity's, and visits to the Grotto for prayers (mostly prayers related to Color War, but prayers nonetheless). Camp was incredible and one of the most important developmental times of my life.

The Head Counselor of Camp Acadia for Boys was Walt Bahr. Walt was a member of the 1948 United States Olympic Soccer Team and the 1950 World Cup team known for its upset of the English National team.

Years later when I moved to Chicago, Walt got me tickets to the World Cup matches at Soldier Field. I invited my friend, Annie Munana, to join me at the USA vs. Spain match, since her folks lived in Madrid, and my friend Mary Ann Doherty to the match vs. Germany. It was around that time that I started making a Christmas card with a highlight from the year as a photo. That year it was a toss-up between a photo of me and my friend Mary Ann Doherty, now Hoey, along with two older German fans. They were both very tall with gray hair, well into their 70s, maybe 80s. Across their chests, they had German flag sashes and, on their heads, crowns with a big soccer ball in the center. Hanging from the points of the crown were smaller soccer balls dangling by string. I was going to have the card read "And these people thought they were going to take over the world?" But, instead, I went with a photo of me in the bleachers at Wrigley Field with a group of about forty priests from a seminary in Evanston in full robes. The caption read: "A good Irish Catholic Girl is never too far away from her Priest or her baseball. Season's Greetings from the bleachers at Wrigley Field!" I had played hooky from work that afternoon and was flying away for the weekend that night. At the airport bar, they had on ESPN. When I looked up, I saw the priests and me front and center as the intro to the show. Busted! I came clean with my boss on Monday, and he laughed.

Camp

Walt Bahr met his wife, Davies Uhler, square dancing at Temple University and they married in 1946. They had three sons and a daughter also named Davies. All four kids were campers at Acadia and Our Lady of Lourdes. Three of them were eventually counselors.

Walt coached soccer at Penn State, and his awesome wife Davies taught assorted physical education classes and ran one of the athletic buildings. Many boys from Acadia have shared that their first crush was on Mrs. Bahr. She was beautiful inside and out and looked after them all summer at camp when their own mothers were not around.

My friend Davies, like me, is the baby of her family. She was on the Orange Team at OLL camp and started as a camper at just four years old. She was quieter than me (not saying much) and a great athlete and wonderful person. She could do a butterfly aerial off the float (we were in awe!) and was often seen in a worn pair of flip-flops. Davies married her Penn State boyfriend, Dan Desiderio in 1982. It was a beautiful wedding on her parents' lawn in Boalsburg, PA, near the university. Soon after, they moved to Dan's hometown of Media, PA, and opened Double D Gymnastics in 1984. Their academy thrived for decades, and they raised their wonderful three sons. No doubt, if they had wanted to, both Davies and Dan could have been on the US Gymnastics team, but instead they taught kids in eastern Pennsylvania how to be the best they could be in a sport they had so much passion for. They recently sold Double D and are enjoying traveling more!

Usually at camp, if there was a big raid, it was done by teenagers, and they got found out and punished. I speak from personal experience, believe me! I had to run the road between the two camps with my partners in crime until we could do it in under eight minutes! It was steep and had tons of rocks. It got to a point where I felt I knew where every rock was on that road, from muscle memory.

During the summer of '77, I asked my mom to bring me a few boxes (like large shirt boxes from Macy's) and some red and orange paint with paint brushes on parents' weekend. She obliged.

I cut out large monster feet in the boxes. One a left foot and one a right foot. Soon after, we snuck over to the boys' camp in the middle of the night. We placed the left foot and then the right foot, alternating them in red and orange team colors, all the way down Acadia's long white dock that ran from the waterfront to the basketball courts.

The day after our boys' camp raid, Mrs. McGrath came into the KP room to speak to the four team captains. Three out of the four of us were on the overnight raid. Anne, the one captain who was not there, kept asking, "What happened? What happened?" The rest of us were completely silent. Mrs. McGrath said, "I thought I would come to the leaders of the division to see if you can find out who did this. Please let me know by the end of the day." Since her daughter, Maureen/Mooie, was in on the raid and Mrs. M. is not a person one should ever try to pull the wool over her eyes, we confessed later that afternoon. And she confessed she knew it was us all along! No one else would be that passionate and organized.

For our punishment, in addition to running the camp road timed, we had to paint the boys' dock white again. Naturally, for our painting task, we wore team colors!

One of the all-time greatest pranks took place in the summer of 1973.

Rich Cariello was a counselor at the boys' camp. He was the Division Leader for Junior boys who were eight and nine years old. We all adored Rich. Not only did Rich date and then marry one of our favorite counselors, Marjorie Loperfido from OLL, but he also set in motion one of the greatest nighttime raids of the girls' camp *ever*! This plan had a specific need for accuracy and was completed with precision, like the Dirty Dozen, but with roughly twenty-four eight- to nine-year-old boys. The counselors involved woke up the boys, tent by tent, in the middle of the night and brought them quietly over to Acadia's mess hall. In the corner, Rich had set up an easel with a map of the girls' camp. This was the first time that these boys had heard of the plan. They were all bleary-eyed when Rich began to explain it and were totally hyped up by the time it ended. He told them they were going to steal over in the middle of the night and would be divided into groups, each led by a counselor. They each had a task. One team would let out the rowboats and canoes, one team would take down the nets at the tennis courts and basketball courts, and another would carry tables, plates, and silverware from the girls' mess hall down to the dock, and then their counselors would row them out to the float to set them up for breakfast.

And Then...

Finally, the last thing they planned was to hang a pair of underwear on the flagpole before leaving. Rich explained that if word got out, they would have to cancel the raid. Secrecy was critical. He said he would never forget the looks on their faces that night. It was amazing that he and the other counselors got them back to sleep. The next morning, they were tired, but excited. And nobody said a word!

A week or so later, on the night of the raid, they woke up the boys around 1:00 a.m. (All of them had kept the plan a secret!) Two by two, they sent them down the tent colony like commandos. Remember, they were eight and nine years old! The counselors collected them all at the end of the colony and started down the camp road with instructions to be prepared to jump into the woods if a car came by. And, sure enough, a car did come by, and they all scrambled into the woods. *Hilarious.*

Meanwhile, at the girls' camp, Marjorie (Rich's girlfriend) was the DL of the Intermediates that year and was helping to clear the way to make sure there was no interference. He recalls she even may have "left" a ladder out at the basketball court to help them take down the nets. The raid went like clockwork. There was nobody around, thanks to Marjorie, and it probably took maybe forty-five minutes or so. When finished, the young boys gathered with their counselors and took off for home. Once again, two by two, they sent them back to their tents exhausted but beaming.

The next day when the girls' camp woke up to reveille and went to Assembly for our daily roll call, there was underwear on the flagpole. When we got to the mess hall for breakfast, there were only a few tables. Word got out quickly that the raid had been

Camp

completed by eight and nine-year-old boys, and everyone reacted well. Mr. Bahr cracked up and even announced it on the Public Address system, of course, just before he played the Music Man record. Mrs. McGrath at OLL was also very cool about it, as she and her husband were big into camp tradition.

Most importantly, the kids were in heaven! Rich told me that many years later at one of our camp reunions at a bar in NYC, two of those boys (obviously now men) went up to him and said that they have never forgotten that night and how special it was. Surely, many of those young boys are now fathers, and I bet they found a way to make their sons or daughters feel that sense of adventure and accomplishment one way or another, remembering that great sense of pride from Camp Acadia.

I cannot remember if the camp closed over the winter of '82 or '83, but it was a crushing blow for so many. Had the parish in NYC not sold, leased, or loaned the camp to be a convent/hermitage/retreat for French nuns, Mooie and I might still be there running up and down the hillside, refereeing badminton and volleyball, going on canoe trips down the Delaware River, singing "Build Me Up Buttercup" into our hairbrushes in the tent colony, waking the camp up to Dan Fogelberg singing "TO THE MORNING" on the loud speaker while swimming laps on Forest Lake, getting psyched for the Apache Relay, sneaking over to the boys camp, and making Hurricane punch at the counselor parties. Camp was my first happy place besides home. Camp opened my eyes to a bigger world.

I made my first two friends from Long Island at camp: Megaera Garvey from Manhasset and Diane from Rockville Center. When

And Then...

we loaded the buses on the last day of camp, for our trip to the Port Authority Bus Terminal at the GW Bridge, Megaera used to tell me how ugly I looked when I cried! My weep is intense, and I can look like an Edvard Munch (*The Scream*) painting quickly. I hated leaving my friends at the end of the summer. Luckily, after camp I typically would go spend another week at Megaera's family's house on the beach in Leetes Island, CT, near Guilford. I can distinctly remember Mrs. Garvey, about six months pregnant at the age of forty-one, diving off the dock into the north shore of Connecticut's Long Island Sound. I always thought she was a rock star. Summer memories were the best!

THE BEST THING about camp was that no one cared if your dad was the CEO of IBM or a garbage man. All we cared about was whether you were fun and nice…and if you were a good athlete, all the better!

Many counselors also left a positive mark on my life from camp! Eunice Howley was Mooie's aunt, who was the Athletic Director and Head of the Waterfront for years. We all loved Margie Ring and Sully (who came up from Brooklyn), Karen and Sue Sarcinella, Anita Higgins, Giggie Breslin, Rosie Pisani, Debby and Kathe Germann, the McGrath sisters, and so many others, including Kate Doyle, who was my tentmate and fellow CIT in the summer of '78. But the one counselor who made the biggest impact on my life was Sue Meaney (now Kapchinske) from Garden City, NY. Sue has a smile and disposition like Maria in *The Sound of Music*. Not only was/is she beautiful with long blonde hair and blue eyes, but she had a positive attitude that was contagious.

In the summer of 1974, I was a Sub Senior and Sue was my Division Leader. There were some girls in the division who had been there a lot longer than I had, who were not always so friendly to an outgoing, relatively newcomer like me. I could not believe it when at the huge bonfire on the last night of camp, she gave me two awards. Mooie, a year my junior, probably won the best athlete trophy for our age group. However, Sue put together a personalized, handmade plaque for an all-around athlete, for me. She also awarded me Best Camper. All these years later, I can still remember how special she made me feel.

Sue skipped camp during the summer of 1977 to be an apprentice with Bonnie Pruden in Stockbridge, Massachusetts. Bonnie Pruden was an American physical fitness pioneer. Her report to Eisenhower on the unfitness of American children as compared with their European counterparts led to the formation of the President's Council on Youth Fitness!

Sue brought back all her knowledge to camp the next year. I can remember dancing to "Day Break" on the front lawn doing exercises and having the time of our lives. In fact, Sue has continued the journey of sharing her skills and passion for physical fitness by running a gymnastics school in the Berkshire Mountains in western Massachusetts.

Sallie Saunders (now Colucci) from Pelham also attended camp. Sallie agrees that Sue was the kind of person/counselor who, just by listening to you, helped you fix your own problems. That is a gift. Sue Meaney, and many others, helped girls at Our Lady of Lourdes Camp navigate that most difficult road of adolescence.

We had great friends at Acadia too whom we spent tons of time with for years, both at camp and over the winter in Long Island,

Brooklyn, Westchester, or Connecticut. Tom Hopkins "Hopper" from Brooklyn; Brian Desmond, also from Pelham; Phil Garvey (Megaera and Adrienne's brother from Manhasset), whose father, Frank Garvey had also gone to Acadia; and others... So many laughs, so many memories, so much fun.

There is not a doubt in my mind that camp molded me into the person I am today, making me confident and daring. I am grateful that so many of these folks are still in my life to this day. Many came to a reunion we organized not far from camp at the Arnold House in the Catskills in 2016, some even from South America! It was a magical weekend and I met campers from both OLL and Acadia who had been there before my time. Though I had never met some of them before, we bonded immediately as we all shared the same passion for and memories from that slice of heaven in the Catskills, a place that will always represent the very best of our childhoods.

And Then... Once again, I was so thankful my mom was able to send me to camp!

Is there a place from your childhood that meant the world to you? Have you had the opportunity to go back and visit? Are you still in touch with the people you met back then? Is there anyone you lost touch with whom you would like to reconnect with? What's holding you back?

With social media, it's getting easier to find someone from your younger years and share a story. Make a list of three to five people from your younger years and do a search to find them. You'll never know what a difference you may have made in *their* life.

Camp

Me, Lisa and Mooie painting the dock as punishment at camp.

Chapter Three

Take Me Home, Country Roads

(Song written by John Denver)

If you had ever asked me in high school where I thought I would go to college, I would have had no idea. But surely, one of the last places I thought I would end up is West Virginia. Though I knew my mom's dad, John Ray Maust, had been born there, I had never visited. My grandfather's obituary from 1973 read, "Born at Bruceton Mills, in Preston County, W. Va., Mr. Maust was reared on a buckwheat farm where his father operated a water powered grist mill. He gained experience in the mining business when he worked for Raney Coal Company in PA in the 1920s. in 1932 he organized Maust Coal & Coke corporation. Maust, at one time the seventh largest coal producer in the USA, was the largest coal shipper on the B&O railroad line and biggest consumer of electrical power from Monongahela Power Company. One of his right-hand men, Joe McQuade, said, 'Mr. Maust was the most honest person I ever knew. He was very generous to people, a hard worker, and a genius. He could recall conversations he had with people almost word for word and was a financial wizard.' He added that Mr. Maust did more for Nicholas County, West Virginia, than any other single man has or probably ever will do."

So, there was that… Even though coal is not a preferred fuel today, back then, it provided jobs and power for thousands of people.

While considering where I wanted to go for the next chapter of my life, I thought that since I love to ski, maybe New England would be a good place to start. I thought that might be a good fit for me as I prepared for my next journey: college. I visited several New England schools that were wonderful, but then got sidetracked on an unexpected adventure.

Since Dad was often in Pittsburgh on business, being in the coal industry, he had me fly down and meet him to go look at a school our family friend Tim Henningsen had told me about. (The Henningsens were an admired Pelham family, and we spent most every Christmas Eve at their house during my childhood.) Tim or "Fletch," as many called him, went to Camp Dewitt in New Hampshire, and met two Bethany College soccer players named Bobby Hill and Drew McConaghy. They told him about their awesome school in the foothills of West Virginia. He gave me a brochure and it looked gorgeous. Along with cute guys in the brochure photos playing frisbee in the quad, they also had a great Communications Department, which I had thought was the direction I should go. My mom encouraged me as well. In the end, I am so grateful that I ended up there. Bethany fit the bill as it is in the country, but it is only forty-five minutes from Pittsburgh, a city I would grow to love.

When Dad and I first visited Bethany, he drove, and I had the map. I love maps. It looked like there was a back road off the highway that was a shortcut to the Bethany Campus. Soon after turning left off Route 844 onto 331, I was thinking, *Where am I?* After passing a shack of a bar I would later fondly visit with friends on Sunday afternoons, called EM's, we passed through some beautiful countryside. The trees were gorgeous, and the sun was shining. Suddenly, we were blocked by a herd of cattle. I looked at my father and said, "I don't think this school really exists. Maybe they made up a fake brochure to punk me?" A little farther up the road, I saw a tall, majestic brick clocktower sticking up through the trees and thought, this must be the place. Soon we passed historical Campbell Mansion. Bethany was founded by Alexander Campbell of the Restoration Movement in 1840. Bethany is a small college of national distinction located on a picturesque and historic 1,300-acre campus in the Northern Panhandle of West Virginia. It was the first institution of higher education and the state's oldest private college.

Although the enrollment was approximately 1500 students, the campus took my breath away, and it had many towering, gorgeous trees and rolling hills, things that make me smile. I remember Mom always saying, "There is nothing wrong with being a big fish in a little pond."

That Friday night, they assigned me to stay at a sorority house on the top of the hill in between two other houses. It seemed like most gals stayed home on a Friday night to study. I was an outgoing high school senior and itching to check out the college scene. I finally convinced someone in the sorority house to take me to Bubba's Bison Inn to explore. I saw and met at least half a dozen people from the Midwest and East

Take Me Home, Country Roads

Coast who were very welcoming and seemed to really enjoy going to Bethany. I thought to myself... *This will work*. It had a nice vibe.

I remember back in Pelham after weighing my options, I walked into the kitchen and said to my mom as she was washing dishes, "I have decided I am going to Bethany College." She turned around from the sink and said, "I know my father is rolling over in his grave with a smile on his face that someone in our family is going back to West Virginia." When friends over the years asked me *why* a girl from New York ended up going to college in West Virginia, my typical response, only half joking, is, "The drinking age was eighteen, I got in, the check cleared, and it was far enough away that my parents could not surprise me on a weekend!" They did also have a great Communications program, and being a small school, we had access to work at the TV or radio station easily. I had the chance to do both.

My first day at Bethany, Tim and I walked into the snack bar called The Barn. An upperclassman named Craig was behind the counter, and I ordered a "Biss-Un Burger." He looked at me, threw a plastic knife, and said "You F*cking freshman, learn your mascot! It is a bye-son!" I replied, totally embarrassed, "Well, I'm from New York and we call them buffaloes!"

In retrospect, I could not imagine *not* having the friends I met at Bethany in my life. Several years after graduating, a New York hospitality industry friend, who had gone to an upstate SUNY school (State University of New York) said to me, "I went to school with 15,000 people and keep in touch with two. You

And Then...

went to school with 1,500 people and keep in touch with 500!" That is just the kind of place Bethany was.

Though my friend Tim ended up pledging Beta, most of the guys I hung out with were from the Kappa Alpha or KA house, Sigma Nu or independents. Dad used to drive down from Pittsburgh whenever he could, and word would spread through campus like wildfire that Mr. McCartney was in town. He would treat my friends to a nice dinner in Wheeling or other nearby towns and then take everyone to Bubba's for cocktails. I remember the bartender, also named Chuck, said to my dad Chuck, "What can I get you?" Dad said, "I'd like a pitcher of Heineken, please." Chuck replied, "We don't sell pitchers of Heineken." Dad said, "I see you have bottles of Heineken Beer and you have pitchers, so if I leave this $20 bill on the bar, can you figure out a way for me to get a pitcher of Heineken?" Next thing you know, a pitcher of Heineken was delivered to our table. What is the saying? "Give the people what they want." When a good tipper like Chuck McCartney is smiling at you, it is hard to say no.

For two years, I ran an alternative Thursday night experience from Bubba's, when the West Liberty College students would hit town. It was called Cabaret at the Barn. We would get local talent and have discounted food and beer. If you could stack enough beer cups to hit the ceiling, you got a free round of beers. I cannot even imagine how much money my father spent trying to get that free round for our gang. That was just how he rolled. Dad was a Phi Kappa Psi from Cornell, but he sure made a lot of friends at Bethany.

Take Me Home, Country Roads

My freshman roommate was Lisa Minard from Fox Chapel, PA, which is a Pittsburgh suburb. One of her high school buddies was named Mark and he also pledged KA. There were a lot of cute soccer players at the KA House, and we ended up spending a lot of time there. Lisa and I both pledged the Zeta Tau Alpha sorority house together. I remember we were late for an open house once because we had gone on a hike through the woods and thought they might blackball us. Later they hosted a talent show, and another Zeta gal named Judy Collins and I were Sony and Cher. I was Cher and made a wig out of shredded black pantyhose that I put on my head, and I wore a long gown and kept flipping my "hair" (a.k.a. pantyhose) behind my shoulders like Cher. "Sony" taped on a mustache, wore a leather coat, and we used toilet paper rolls with tinfoil balls on top as microphones and we sang, "I Got You Babe." I hoped they felt anyone who was willing to make such fools out of themselves, in such a big way, deserved to be in the house. Soon thereafter, I was the tenured social chairman.

The same monster feet prank I pulled at camp, I also coordinated at Bethany, incorporating shamrocks into the artwork. After I was made the social chairman of my sorority, I enlisted the help of some of my fellow sisters and on St. Patrick's Day Eve, we painted green and white monster feet from the top of the hill, down to the cafeteria, along with some shamrocks. It looked like a sea of clovers when everyone woke up on March 17th. (It all ran off after it rained, but people seemed to get a kick out of it and there was no proof of who did it...though I am sure many suspected!) I remember my ZTA friend Evelyn del Cerro helping me with the green paint prank and saying to me, "If I get kicked out of college for painting Irish clovers and green monster feet for St. Patrick's Day, my Puerto Rican mother will kill me!"

I used to wear all green and pass out xeroxed copies of great Irish sing-along songs in the cafeteria on March 17th. It has always been a favorite holiday of mine and I have been to Ireland twenty times over the years. It was not until this last trip in September of 2019 on my way home from Dubrovnik that through Ancestry.com, I found a connection to some distant cousins on my dad's side in Dublin! My buddy Conor McAuliffe joined me for lunch with Noleen Curran and her son Niall, who found me on Ancestry.com and made the connection after the DNA match. They were great and walked me around the area of town where my great grandfather had lived before shipping off to NYC.

My mom has a pillow in our living room that reads: *There are two types of people in this world. Those who are Irish and those who wish they were!*

My junior year, in the Fall of 1981, I ended up participating in a semester abroad at Wagner College in Bregenz, Austria. It was an unforgettable experience. We had classes on Tuesday, Wednesday, and Thursday and were usually on a train most every Thursday night to discover another country. I lived with Frau Boch in a cute white house maybe ten minutes from the school at Schlossberg Strasse 3. My housemates were Carol from Staten Island, NY, Gail from Minnesota, and Wannee from

Thailand. Upon arrival, we drew straws to see who got the singles and who had to share. I won the first draw and selected a lovely room with a large armoire, a cove for my bed near a window, and a skylight in the ceiling, so it was very bright and cheerful. We all had big fun together. I remember teaching Wannee some Irish drinking songs I knew from camp and hearing her sing them with her Thai accent was hilarious. She eventually married and moved to Chicago and joined me on my balcony a few years back for a catch up and a laugh!

Being abroad introduced me to a much more international group of people. And these people from around the globe had worries I never even considered or imagined. I became friends with a guy on our program named Rashid from Iran. One night, several months into the school semester, he and I were talking in the school social room. He said to me, "Margie, what would you do if you thought you were going to be killed?" I said that I had never really thought about it because I lived in the USA and had a stable life. Rashid shared that he had paid $10,000 to be snuck over the Iran border. Iran was at war with Iraq and the American hostages had recently been released.

This was the time of the Ayatollah and revolution. Rashid found out that a guy he knew, who had escaped the same way Rashid had, had been tracked down in Turkey and sent back to Iran. Rashid himself had gone from Iran to Turkey to Germany to Austria. He signed up for two semesters at Wagner College in Bregenz, as he had been assured the best way to get into the United States was with a student visa. When he found out that the other guy had been sent back to Iran, he was worried that he might be next. The punishment could be jail time or execution, neither option one he cared to explore. He was afraid, and I don't blame him.

Others started joining us in the social room and were in awe listening to his story and really wanted to help. We figured he needed to get out of Europe and hopefully into the USA as soon as possible. Remember, we were very young. I suggested that he should marry one of us in the group and I volunteered if it would save his life. I figured I could marry this kind soul and get him into the USA as a citizen and then he would be safe. Then we could quietly get a divorce. I made a Christmas tape for my family that I mailed home saying as much. My sister said my family practically fell off their chairs when I got to that part on the tape. "You could hear a pin drop," she said. But a few sentences later, I shared that Dr. Mittelstadt (who ran the program) caught wind of our plan, pulled some strings, and helped to get Rashid safely into the USA. Although several of my classmates were disappointed, as they wanted to be bridesmaids. Rashid finished up at Wagner College in Staten Island, and then moved to the Detroit suburbs and eventually, in 1987, relocated to California. He is happily married with two children and owns his own hair salon. He loves California! We just spoke on the phone for the first time in forty years and it felt like it was yesterday. Can't wait to connect in person on my next trip to LA!

One evening, a group of about five of us were having dinner in Bregenz, and we met an elderly German man and his wife and started chatting with them at the next table. He heard our accents and shared that he had been to America before. We asked him, "Where?" He said, Texas, Alabama, and a few other southern states. We asked if he had been there on vacation, and he said, "No, I was a prisoner of war in WWII." Our jaws dropped. Up until that moment, we did not even know that we'd had POWs from Europe on US soil during that war. He said that he was treated very well, and we continued chatting with him and his lovely wife.

The focal point of our social life in Bregenz revolved around S'Eck, which was the corner bar and in fact means "Corner." Though we often traveled, when in town, we usually started or ended our nights there. We knew the owners, Doris and Ferdinand, well and they were always very kind to the American students.

When my parents flew over to visit, we ended up playing a drinking game at the S'Eck. One rule of the game was that every time you pointed, you had to drink a big sip of your beer. My dad thought this was very funny. Every time my dad saw me go to the bathroom, he noticed the door said Damen, which means Ladies. However, the next day he was driving my mom to Belgium to tour the battlefields he'd fought on during the war, and at one point, he had to go to the bathroom. He stopped at a gas station and was trying to think of the German word for bathroom, but all he could think of was DAMEN from when he saw me heading to the ladies' room. He was trying to explain to the manager of the gas station that he had to go to the bathroom by grabbing the waistband of his pants and saying DAMEN in his NY accent. Well, this did not go the way he planned; the man assumed he was looking for a hooker and kicked him out of the gas station.

And Then...

We had great tours of beautiful cities across Europe. I remember meeting Senator Ted Kennedy from Massachusetts and his son, Teddy, in the parking lot outside Chartres Cathedral in France, which was my favorite church. We saw a chauffeur put a pizza box in the back of a beautiful Rolls Royce and took photos in front of it like it was our car. Then, Kennedy walked up to the car and started laughing. He was friendly, and we took a photo with him and his son, too. Our trip to Paris was fun with the group, except that at our hotel, some students had their passports stolen from their room when we were down at breakfast. Our wonderful director, Dr. James Mittelstadt, spoke to the manager of the hotel and got it all squared away, and the passports were returned before we headed out on the bus to tour Paris for the day. I do not know how the conversation played out, but it was not his first rodeo. Doc knew what he was doing. He was tall, found with a pipe in his mouth more times than not, and had run the program for years. He was well liked and appreciated by all. He reminded us of a taller Bob Newhart because he was so laid back.

After our Christmas ski trip, but before my first ever trip to Ireland on New Year's Eve, my friend Lisa Pinto from Bethany invited me to visit her in Paris. She had been studying there for a semester and had come to visit me in Bregenz earlier in the autumn. Again, this was way before cell phones. It was a long journey from Bregenz to Paris on trains and then cabs into the night. I remember my cab driver getting lost and driving around the block about four times till we realized we were where we needed to be from the start. The fact that I do not speak French and he did not speak English could have had something to do with that! I was so excited to find my friend that I raced out of the car, and somehow my sleeping bag came unraveled and was flapping behind me like a Chinese parade dragon. I ran up the stairs and knocked on Lisa's apartment door over and over, but she never answered. Finally, her neighbor opened his door and said, "Lisa Go America." We must have gotten our wires crossed on the date of my arrival. Again, no emails or cell phones back then. So, heartbroken, I put my sleeping bag down in her hallway and slept, praying I would be safe and alive in the morning.

I returned to Bethany in 1982 and quickly got caught up in the men's BC Soccer team and their run to the NCAA Division III championships. It was beyond exciting! Admittedly, and a little embarrassingly, after just traveling all over Europe for a semester, it felt weird returning to our little oasis after just experiencing so many international adventures across Europe. I felt like, "What am I doing playing pool in Wellsburg after just being at the Eiffel Tower?" But then, I realized that this was the normalcy of life, and I was glad to be able to return to a place that was so laid back. Having the awesome soccer team to follow and cheer for quickly bought me back down to earth.

After our soccer team beat Denison in the Great Lakes Regional competition, we played Ohio Wesleyan. The clock ran out on the 0–0 tie, but we had our penalty kick superstar Tim Lovell in, and he came through for us, blocking three out of five penalty shots. Allan Barnes scored the winning goal and

And Then...

was named MVP of the tournament. Then at the end of the season, our win over OWU meant that we would be playing Wheaton College from outside of Chicago in the NCAA quarterfinal game. I organized a bus to take us to Chicago, leaving Bethany on Friday night and arriving at Wheaton the next morning a few hours before the game began. I remember when we saw signs for Chicago, we all broke out in song singing, "Chicago, Chicago, that toddling town. Chicago, Chicago, I'll show you around, you'll love it!" Little did I know, I would eventually end up calling Chicago home years later.

At Wheaton College you are not allowed to drink, dance, smoke, or swear. This was a far cry from Bethany where, let's just say, we were not rule oriented! We were not looking pretty after our long drive.

When we arrived after the all-night bus ride from West Virginia, some of our players (the team flew together from Pittsburgh to O'Hare) saw us through the cafeteria windows and waved us in, telling the cafeteria staff that we were assistant managers. Pancakes tasted pretty good around then.

The game was played in a strong windstorm. Fortunately, Bethany prevailed and afterward, we physically covered up the letters of the school so instead of Wheaton College, it said, *EAT OLLE*. Pretty sure their dean wrote our dean asking us to never return.

After a great win at Wheaton, Bethany hosted Scranton University in the semifinal game, which we won. Bethany was to host the championship game because UNC Greensboro did not have a regulation field. However, the NCAA Committee arranged for the game to be played at Guilford College instead of Bethany. A great disappointment re: location of game, but the team and a large fanbase made plans to travel to Greensboro, NC, for the national championship game. I booked my flight immediately and many friends did as well.

As the team traveled to North Carolina, the college super van broke down on the way to the airport. Coach Cunningham convinced a tow truck driver to break from protocol and to tow the super van with all twenty-six players and coaches to the airport. JC shared that he wished they had cell phones in 1982 to provide witness to the Bethany soccer team departing from the van attached to the tow truck. Not a good omen for what followed.

The cold weather was a factor in the final game, and unfortunately, so was the referee. Though we did not win the national championship that year, the 1982 National Finalist season provided positive groundwork for the 1994 Division III National Championship title for Bethany. It gave us all great joy and pride to go along for the ride!

Bethany was one of four schools I knew about in the USA that required you to take Senior Comprehensives. This was an oral and written exam where you had to test on four years of your major.

Bob and Helen Mitchell were longtime residents of Bethany, and both worked at the college. I knew them because I played on the Bethany softball team with their daughter Beth. She was short stop and I played left field. We became fast friends the moment we met. To study for my Senior Comprehensives, the Mitchells cleaned out their attic and put a bed and table and lamp in there for me so I could live with them over January term and would have quiet time to prepare. They were so gracious. Talk about cramming four years into a month! I was nervous. Though extremely stressful, it fortunately all worked out in the end!

The Ornithology class, which I thought was going to be an easy A… NOT SO MUCH! The final exam was ten dead stuffed birds. My guesses were Bird #1, this bird is dead; Bird #2, this is a dead bird with spots; Bird #3, this bird will never fly again. To this day, the only birds I can readily recognize are Cardinals, Blue Jays, and Orioles. If you're not a baseball fan, these are the mascots of the St. Louis, Toronto, and Baltimore Major League Baseball teams. Over the years, however, I would mail postcards to Dr. Buckelew, who taught that class, of birds from around the world in my travels.

Even now, when I drive back to Bethany on an autumn day, cruising down the long winding hill on Rt. 88, I get goosebumps because it looks like God took a big box of Fruit Loops cereal and sprinkled it on the rolling hills. Truly so beautiful, it takes your breath away. Things that make me smile have always included winding roads, sunshine, the smell of grass, the sound of wind, and an abundance of colorful trees.

In 2019, I was invited to the Ann W. Trombadore Women & Leadership Symposium at Bethany College. During the two days, I met some wonderful students, reconnected with some old friends, and heard some terrific alumni speakers, including South Carolina Supreme Court Justice Kaye Hearn.

The organizer, Scarlett Foster, said, "I think the best thing is it's important, as a woman, to always be advancing other women." Also, an inspirational speaker who was at Bethany with me, Kathy Taylor Tucker, got folks fired up. Then they had another lady who asked if there was something you wanted to do but needed to make the first step. I had been dreaming about going on a Global Scavenger Hunt for years but needed to get things lined up at work. She inspired me to move things along, and I did.

In 2015, I got a random email from Bill Chalmers, the creator of The Global Scavenger Hunt, and I was pumped to figure out when I could make that trip happen. The premise is that they take fifteen teams of two people to ten countries in three weeks for adventures that you won't know about until you arrive. I needed to speak to my boss and make sure I had her blessing to take a three-week sabbatical in April 2020. I did. She said yes, and plans were moving forward. In fact, conversations were underway with some Bethany folks to speak at a future Bethany Women's Leadership weekend about my adventure, but that would have to wait, since the dream trip I had saved up for financially for five years got canceled due to COVID-19, just like everything else in all our lives.

I am hopeful that eventually, it will be rescheduled when the world gets back to normal! The not knowing where we were going or what our assignments would be in each country was the part that intrigued me the most. Kathleen Wood was go-

And Then...

ing to be my traveling companion. She is one of the smartest women I know. Kathleen and her sister Sue Tierno, own Suzy Swirl (frozen yogurt) in Illinois and are both incredible women I admire. Kathleen and I were confident we would crush this. Initially, I thought I was too old, until I shared that concern with Pamela Chalmers, the coordinator of the Global Scavenger Hunt, and she told me she thought that was funny since last year's winners were sixty-eight. I said, "I AM IN!"

Bethany has other famous alumni, including Academy Award-winning actress Frances McDormand. Other notable alumni are actor and director William H. Macy, and Tom Poston the comedian, though all before my time.

There was a character who worked at Bethany named Larry Hummel. He worked in the maintenance department. Larry was a disheveled-looking guy whose sneakers and clothes were tied together with safety pins. His birthday was March 12th and I used to have little birthday get-togethers for him in the cafeteria. I felt bad for Larry. Larry wandered around the campus at all hours with an imaginary lawnmower. I had no idea where he lived, but we assumed it must be a box in the woods. There were rumors that he was a millionaire, but I never believed them. We thought he was blowing his nose in the newspapers he would pull out of the garbage, not reading the stock market. One day, he stopped me in the cafeteria and said, "Marge, you're from New York, aren't you?" I said, "Yes." He replied, "They find that Lindbergh baby yet?"

Larry died in the mid 1980s after I had graduated, and my mom called me at work in NYC after listening to her favorite radio show, Paul Harvey and The Rest of the Story. They had just run a story saying that Lawrence Hummel from Bethany College had died and indeed left approximately one million dollars to the school that employed him for thirty years raking leaves, doing yard and janitorial work.

Years later, on my first trip to Canada since Expo '67, my Bethany friend, Paul Hayward, picked me up at the Toronto airport. Paul was a part of the Bethany soccer excitement in 1982, but his eligibility had run out, so he was a student assistant. I was so excited to be in Canada for the first time as an adult and Paul said, "Hey, the Bethany soccer team is playing Freemont College in NY. Why don't we drive down for the game today?" Well, I had just flown up from LaGuardia, and returning to NY was not on the list of things I thought I would do that day, but we went and had a great time. I remember he bought a six pack of beer and had it in the trunk returning to Canada. Going back over the border, most people when asked if they were bringing anything into the country would just say, "No", but Paul with his floppy blond hair and huge grin honestly said, "I have a six pack in the trunk." The border patrolman just smiled and waved us through.

One of the things that drew people to Paul was his charm and fun spirit. He was kind and silly, and once I got to know his family, I saw why. What struck me the most about Paul once

And Then...

I really got to know him was that he accepted all people. I always try to see the good in all people, but sometimes, I give up if I do not feel like they are worth it. Paul felt everyone was worth it. I try to be more like him in that way, but it is not always easy.

Paul lost his battle with cancer in February 2015, and his family and friends coordinated a Celebration of Life in Florida in the spring. Hundreds of people showed up and paid tribute to our friend. We all believe that Paul lived longer than they expected after being diagnosed with stage four cancer, because he wanted to spend every possible moment on this earth that he could with his beloved son Jackson. A bench sits in front of his family's condo on the beach on AMI that reads:

> Paul "Ace" Hayward 1959-2015
> He leaves us with a legacy of
> love, kindness, compassion, and
> everlasting friendship
> Rest in Peace
> *Smiledeep*

I have a blue stone from Paul that is with a collection in my home of stones and shells that I value for the memories they hold. Another trademark of Paul were his red sneakers. To me they scream, LIVE YOUR LIFE OUT LOUD! The last time I saw him was on Anna Maria Island in Florida, where he lived the last few years of his life. It was over New Year's 2014 turning into 2015…just months before he died, and he gave me a pair of red Keds sneakers at his sister Carolann's condo on the beach. I *smiledeep* every time I put them on. Carolann's friendship has been a gift in my life, and we have grown so very close. When one door closes, another one opens. She and her husband, Jim Malenfant, are the epitome of Paul's kindness, and she and Paul look so much alike that when I am with her, it almost feels like he is there with us too.

There is a reason that at almost every Bethany College wedding I have attended, the band or DJ plays, "Take Me Home, Country Roads" or all of us just break out in song ourselves with no backup. We don't really need it after all.

And Then... I remember how grateful I am that I ended up at that little, beautiful school in the foothills of West Virginia. Even though I was not the best student for 5 a.m. birdwatching, I still connected with my teacher. I think since I used to give people rides on the back of my skis down to class in the winter, he liked me anyway.

Sometimes our smallest efforts have the greatest impact on others. How could you step up and do a little more than you currently are? Could you help someone in need you would normally walk by? Could you share a compliment with someone who appears to be having a bad day? Giving back to the world either by donations or volunteering for the underprivileged is a great way of celebrating the circle of life.

And Then...

Allen Tait, second from left and Sally Esposito, far right after Bethany defeated Wheaton College in the soccer playoffs.

With Ted Kennedy and his son Teddy in the parking lot of Chartres Cathedral in Chartres, France, 1981.

Susan and I in Sydney at the start of the 2000 Olympics.

Chapter Four

The Lottery of Life

My friend Susan Keary and I met in 1984. I knew who she was before she knew me. I was commuting to NYC via Metro North from Pelham after college. She was this stunning woman who was regularly on the train platform while I was waiting to commute to Grand Central Station. In the cold weather, she often wore a gorgeous fur coat that I thought was spectacular! She had (still does) bright blue eyes and an awesome smile.

All along in life, I pretty much figured I would find my way into the hospitality industry due to my love of bringing people together to have fun! In fact, in the spring of 1984 when I met Susan, I was organizing a Bethany College reunion on a booze cruise that sailed from Fort Slocum Park in New Rochelle.

Commuters to the city on Metro North often called Peltown Taxi for a ride to the Pelham Train Station. They would pick up several passengers at various homes and take them the few miles to the station as a group of strangers. One day, my friend John was driving for Peltown and he picked me up. Then we picked up Susan. I did not know her name, but when she got into the cab, I realized it was the stunning Irish gal from the train station platform. She was friendly. When she heard me trying to get John, the cab driver, to come to the Bethany Booze Cruise, she asked what I was talking about. Though it was a college reunion, I had many friends going to the party from camp and Pelham, as well as college friends and their friends. All were welcome. I invited Susan, but she had plans that weekend and said, "I'll come next year!" After our cab introduction, we would often sit together on the train, chatting, in the mornings. Soon thereafter, I noticed that she was not wearing her wedding ring anymore. She shared with me on the train that she was going through a divorce. I said I was sorry, but that she should meet two of my guy friends from college who lived in New Jersey. Susan was apprehensive but decided to put her worries aside and agreed to join us. We met my Bethany buddies Jamie Trainor and Tom Taylor at Puglia's in Little Italy in NYC. If you have never been there before… it is a classic. Located on Hester Street in lower Manhattan's Little Italy, the wine is fair, but they pour it freely. You sit at big picnic tables with your group, or they sometimes combine groups. The food is served in large portions and is very affordable. The true value is the atmosphere of 100% PURE FUN AND LAUGHTER. There might be Conga lines through the kitchen, a man with a parrot on his shoulder for photos, people chanting, "This is Table #1, Where is table #2?" If you can't have fun at Puglia's, you can't have fun! Needless to say, a great time was had by all, and wonderful new friendships were made.

The greatest gift Susan has given me (besides her friendship) is a book she made for my 50th birthday, which we celebrated with friends and family in Napa Valley, my happy place! She solicited input from friends and family across the globe and asked them to send a photo and share what our friendship means to them. It was beyond thoughtful. I am so grateful to have that beautiful book to look at from time to time. It always makes me smile. Additionally, I wear a necklace every day that she got me for my birthday probably twenty years ago. It reads, *EMBRACE LIFE!* We are both very good at that, for sure.

Over the years, Susan and I have traveled together to Greece, Cabo San Lucas, Mexico, Napa several times, Scottsdale, West Virginia, Las Vegas, Baltimore, San Francisco, New Orleans, and rafted down the Grand Canyon. We are both huge sports fans and have attended the MLB All-Star game in Denver, spent many sunny days in the bleachers at Wrigley Field, and attended the World Series several times at Yankee Stadium. We enjoyed some great tailgating days at Meadowlands for the Giants and Jets.

However, our greatest adventure was in 2000 when we went to the Olympics in Sydney, Australia. I treated her to my frequent flier miles, and she ended up getting us complimentary tickets to the Opening Ceremonies!

We were at the swimming preliminaries in Sydney and met up (by chance) with the family of Tom Dolan, who was from Virginia and was competing in the prelims. They all had hats on with American flags that said, *TOM*. Tom won that race and was headed to the finals. We did not have tickets to the finals. However, Tom's family was kind enough to give us two extra tickets. Susan and I were not sitting together at the venue, but we were filled with excitement for Tom and his family. The next day, Tom Dolan ended up winning the gold medal in the men's 400-meter individual medley and set a new world record in the final. We were so excited, and I had my American flag draped around me, and my emotions got the best of me. Without thinking, I just

The Lottery of Life

hopped over the railing and ran down poolside to celebrate with the swimmers. It was mayhem. I did not even think of *not* doing it. No one stopped me or told me I could not be there. This was clearly pre 9/11.

I remember once, I said to Susan how great it would be to win the lottery and have enough money to do anything, and she replied, "You know what, Margie, we have already won the *Lottery of Life,* being born into our families, so we can't really ask for anything more."

And Then... I realized how right she was. Though we have no control over how or where we come into this world, when you are born into a loving family, and have amazing friends, you are always rich enough.

Blood does not always make up a family. Who are your friends who could make up your family? Or neighbors? Or those who make you feel safe and happy? I truly know how lucky I was to grow up the way I did and I never take it for granted.

Thinking back on the different stages and ages of your life, did your "family" change? Have you ever experienced how your friends can become like family for you?

And Then...

Celebrating my brother's birthday with my sister Mary.

It is OK to Be a BOZO!

Sydney embraces BOZOS!

Chapter Five

It is OK to Be a BOZO!

My parents, Charles George McCartney, and Joan Dorothy Maust, met at a party in Pelham in late 1950. My father had grown up in Brooklyn, New York, and was adopted at birth by Charles and Edith McCartney. Years later, I would find out through Ancestry.com that he really was a McCartney all along! We all look very Irish, so I figured when growing up that if we were not actually McCartneys, we were certainly O'Learys or Murphys! Back in the 1920s, if someone unmarried in a family got pregnant, often they would give the child to another family member to raise. This must have been the case with Dad's family. His parents both died before he turned fourteen, and in his mother's will, Edith McGuiness McCartney bequeathed her only son to her best friend Edith Burns. Edith soon moved him from Brooklyn to Center Ave in New Rochelle, NY, in Westchester County. Edith Burns, originally from Austria, opened a dress shop in Brooklyn. She had been married to a man who was killed in the Battle of Marne in WWI. He never got the chance to meet their only child, a daughter named Marjorie. Dad and Marjorie became family because of two best friends named Edith. These important women in my dad's life are how I ended up getting the name Marjorie Edith.

It is OK to Be a BOZO!

My folks had their first official date on New Year's Eve 1950, and two weeks later they were engaged. Six months later, they were married. I recently found the Herald Tribune announcement dated Jan 21, 1951. It was probably in the cards all along that my dad, now a WWII veteran, would go work for my grandfather, his father-in-law, selling coal. But, to prove himself, he continued to work for Union Carbide for several more years before joining Maust Coal and Coke Corporation.

Our favorite story from that time was when he had to give a speech at the Waldorf Astoria in Manhattan, in front of about 500 Union Carbide employees. He got up, stood tall, walked up to the microphone, and confidently announced, "Our company is branching out like the testicles of an octopus." The whole room cracked up laughing! When he got home, he said to my mom, "Joan, it is the testicles of an octopus, isn't it?" She said, "No you dope, it's the tentacles!" He said, "Well, they loved me."

Even crazier, about eight or so years ago, my friend Beth from New Orleans was working at the NOLA Intercontinental Hotel. The phone rang in the Sales Department, and she happened to pick it up and it was a man from Galveston, Texas. He said he wanted to organize a military reunion at the Intercon NOLA. He had heard that Intercontinental Hotels gave good rates to the military. He also said that he worked for Union Carbide. Well, my friend Beth *loved* that story about my father, so she said to the man on the phone, "Does the name Chuck McCartney ring a bell to you?" He said that it did, but he did not know why. She shared that about sixty-five years ago, Chuck was working for Union Carbide and was giving a speech at the Waldorf Astoria in NYC when he got on stage at a Union Carbide meeting and said, "Our company is branching out…" And then the man on the other end of the phone interrupted her and said, "Like the testicles of an octopus! It's company lore!"

Beth called me in Chicago to tell me that story. I was beaming. I immediately called my mom in New York to tell her that story and her response was perfect. Though Dad died in 2005 on their 54th wedding anniversary, she said, "Your father would love that story because people remembered him…even if it was for being a BOZO!"

And then…I smiled even bigger because she was so right. Everyone likes to be remembered.

Our Dad was certainly memorable, even if it was sometimes for being a BOZO.

Fortunately, my kindergarten pal, Heather's, birthday is in the first quarter of the year in March, so she had already turned seventeen and had her driver's license when we were seniors in high school. My brother Drew was back from college and had a green mustang convertible in the driveway.

There was a bar in New Rochelle called the Barge. It was the first bar I ever went to. Though they checked your ID, it was easy to distract them, and you could probably get in with a photo of your cat.

It is OK to Be a BOZO!

Heather was over at our house and no one else was home. It was late in the day, and we decided to "borrow" Drew's car for a joy ride. We drove down to the Barge on the water in New Rochelle. It felt cool driving there in a convertible. They had a new bouncer that day and we had no luck getting in. We just decided to go back home when it started to rain. The top was down, and we had no idea how to put it up. Looking like two bozos, we drove back up Pelhamdale Avenue in a convertible, in the rain, laughing the whole time! It is the little things in life that make you happy!

After college, I worked at Doremus Advertising on Wall Street and then for The Sporting Goods Dealer (Owned by the Sporting News) on 2nd Ave, a short walk from Grand Central Station. There, my boss was a hilarious Italian man named Gene. He was a ton of fun and a great boss and lived one train stop away from Pelham, in Mt. Vernon. It was always interesting to fly with Gene because he was petrified of flying. He had to hold on to the arm rests during takeoff, sweating, with his eyes closed.

I remember we went to a Sporting Goods trade show in Atlanta once. My college friend, Tom Weber, also a super fun guy, had moved down there soon after Bethany from Washington, PA, and was enjoying life. During a break in the show, Gene and I met Tom for lunch. We laughed so hard that we cried. We all had a million stories to share. It must have seemed like a BOZO convention! I went into the ladies' room toward the

And Then...

end of the meal, and a woman came up to me while I was washing my hands. She said, "May I tell you something?" I hesitantly said, "Yes." She said, "I have to tell you that I am very jealous of you and your two gentlemen friends laughing all through your lunch. I wish I were sitting at your table!" I told her I knew I was lucky and had we not been leaving; I would have invited her to join us.

My first DMC, Destination Management Company, job was with a company called Safari's in NYC. I did not even know this was a profession when I was younger, but I sort of fell into it. My buddy Heather McLeod's older sister, Diane McLeod McCurdy, was leaving her job to be a Marketing Manager for a DMC in NYC called Safari's. While visiting her parents' house in Pelham, she saw a flier on the kitchen table that I had put together for a Saint Patrick's Day Limousine Race Scavenger Hunt and said to Heather, "Margie should really get involved in the hospitality industry. She would be perfect for the company I am joining. Let me see if I can set up an interview." And the rest, as they say, is history.

I met the director of the Safari's DMC-NYC office, Randy Smith, for my interview in 1985. I was offered the job. I knew immediately that we would be great friends and we still are to this day. Through Randy, I met my friend Amos, who suggested that I move to Chicago back in the day. I will never be able to thank him enough! He told me that I would love it there. He said, "It is a great sports town with lots of fun people, lots of

It is OK to Be a BOZO!

Irish people, and the scene near Wrigley Field, where I live, is awesome. You would fit right in!" It certainly worked out for me!

I became the Program Manager at Safari's. We worked long hours, making little money. Often in the fall, we might get a day off every few weeks.

Fall Foliage Tours up the St. Lawrence River were very popular for Royal Viking and Royal Cruise lines. At that time, we coordinated all their logistics for NYC. Our office walls at Safari's on 51st Street had maps of Newark, LaGuardia, and Kennedy airports taped all over the place. It looked like we were planning the invasion of Normandy with all the arrows going everywhere on the graphs and charts on our office walls. We had probably 100 staff people working for us at ten dollars an hour and flew other Safari's employees in from around the country to help manage these weekly programs with people arriving at three airports. It was a chore getting them into NYC to two different hotels, taking them on tours of the city, and then the following day, getting them to the pier to start their cruise tours. Many a night, I was greeting delayed flights at Kennedy or Newark, exhausted and trying to decipher whether the guest was staying at the Intercontinental in NYC or the Hilton. The color-coded luggage tags were…wait for it…pink and peach! Really? Not sure who came up with that great idea, but it is very hard to tell them apart, especially in often dimly lit, crowded baggage claim areas with restless people jockeying for position all around you. One night, very late, I found a large suitcase in the back of the shuttle as we were about to call it quits. I looked at the tag and realized it was someone from our group who would be leaving on the cruise in the morning. I took the bag and put it in a cab and went to the Intercontinental Hotel in midtown, found out the couple's room, and bought it up to their door and woke them up at about 1 a.m. to hand deliver it to them. I will never forget, the man gave me a $100 bill and said, "THANK YOU SO MUCH, you have saved our trip."

One day during these large excursions, we were picking people up after the foliage tour at the Pier on the upper west side. The ships arrive and they are supposed to disembark the passengers to coincide with the times of their flights. People with flights at 11 a.m. get off first, then noon, etc.

We had buses lined up with the names of the airlines and airports outside. Most of these travelers were elderly and many packed *two* trunks for their Fall Foliage tours up the St. Lawrence River! We were simultaneously getting hundreds of people from the airports into the city for a night, so there was constantly many people coming and going fast. They all seemed to have tons of luggage. We would finish with one manifest and jump right into the next one.

On this day, for whatever reason, the captain must have just said, "GOODBYE," as if he was leaving and opened the departure doors of the ship. It was insane! Oceans of people, many with gray hair and tons of luggage were yelling for help and swarming the bus area. We had lots of signage up for each airline and each airport, but there were so many people, I am not sure who could see what! I was trying to help get as many bags on each bus as we could, so I crawled into the baggage

It is OK to Be a BOZO!

compartment under one bus, trying to pack everything as tightly as possible. At that moment, a man threw a big suitcase into the bin. It hit me in the face, and I started bleeding from my lip. Talk about feeling like a BOZO! We needed to get more help, so I raced for the elevator to get to command central because it was a mess. I was trying to call from my walkie talkie on the elevator when the elevator broke down! There were no cell phones back then. Our office leader who had been flown in from San Francisco was saying from his walkie talkie with his British accent, "Margie, I can't hear you. You are breaking up. Call from a land line."

Finally, I wedged my fingers between the doors and slowly pulled the elevator doors open. I have heard about people getting strength from another power when things are crazy, and this was for sure that. When the doors opened, I jumped down from the elevator to the sidewalk, probably four feet. I was dressed like Julie from *The Love Boat* in a khaki skirt, white blouse, blue blazer, and red, white, and blue scarf. I was maybe twenty-five years old at the time, and I toppled slightly but got up and right then, a man had a heart attack in front of me! I am not making ANY OF THIS UP. We finally maneuvered an ambulance in to get him to the hospital where he survived. We eventually got all the people on all the buses to all the airports.

Exhausted, our NY staff limped over to a burger joint/bar on the west side, and we ordered *several strong drinks* and dinner before going home to crash. I think it was that afternoon when I figured that I needed to get out of the DMC business for good. After all, I'm not that much of a BOZO, but I would say it had been a BOZO Day! (But ironically, I ended up making it my career!)

During the Professional Convention Managers Association Annual Convening Leaders conference in Nashville in 2018, I got a phone call.

It was from an old friend who shared that he had had a stroke that affected his vision. His wife was away down south taking care of her mother for a year. I wanted to make sure I could do something nice for him. I said that when I got back to Chicago, I would pick him up for dinner and a movie the next Friday night.

My husband Gary and I share a car, but I was lucky to have a friend in the building who let me use her car when Gary had our Nissan at work. Margaret O'Hara and I met on the elevator of our building, Lake Park Plaza, years ago when she overheard me saying I needed a cat sitter. She was kind enough to chime in that she could help me out and so our friendship began. Margaret is a petite, spitfire, British lady who is always dressed to the nines.

Margaret has a black Oldsmobile Cutlass. The last time I had borrowed it, it had been parked upstairs in our parking garage in the third spot on the right. Mind you, I am not really a car person. Radio, radiator, it is all the same to me. On the night I was going to take my friend to dinner and a movie, I went to that same spot and got in the black car, started the engine, and drove off. Margaret had left a note with the parking garage years ago allowing us to take her car anytime we needed it. Off I went to dinner and a movie with my friend. We grabbed dinner at a pizza place I like, and then saw Hugh Jackman in *The Greatest Showman* and loved it. I dropped my friend off at his house and drove back home. I pulled into the garage and told the parking attendants that Margaret's car was back. They looked at each other, looked at the car, and looked at me, and said, "That's not Margaret's car!"

I was mortified and said, "Whose car is it then?" They said, "Bobby D'Onofrio." I didn't know who that was, because we live in a large high rise. I said, "Well, I hope he is nice!"

The next morning, I asked the front desk to give my cell phone number to Bobby. I knew they would not give his to me without permission, but I wanted to go to his apartment and apologize face to face to him and his wife Rena. I recognized him right away from seeing him around the building for years and he was always super friendly, with a cool thick mane of gray hair and a big friendly smile. Plus, he was a big Cubs fan and always chatted to me and my husband Gary in the laundry room about the baseball season. We just never knew his name! They totally understood that it was not deliberate, just an innocent mistake. I did not know I was stealing his car! They checked the car and there was no damage, nothing was missing, and it had only been driven a few miles. Though he did say, "I don't know how you could get a Honda mixed up with a Cutlass?" I said it was dark, the cars are both black, it was in the same spot as the last time I borrowed it, and they both had the same interior color, and he had just two keys on the keychain, just like Margaret's car. We laugh about it to this day.

And then... I thought, who knew I could make a new friend by being a BOZO, and accidentally stealing his car?

When my Pelham High School buddy, Sal Candido, got married, it was June of 1998. That same weekend I had flown an old college friend into NY from Chicago because her father had recently died, and she was sad. I figured I could share my awesome dad with her and bought her a plane ticket to New York for Christmas. She and my friend Susan Keary kept my folks company in the afternoon and through dinner, while I went to Sal's wedding in the next town over. I was meeting them at McLintocks Pub in North Pelham after the wedding, which was held at the Surf Club on Davenport Avenue in New Rochelle.

While driving, I found traffic completely jammed. I realized it was prom season, plus the Mets were playing the Yankees that weekend. I was just about to put my car in reverse and back up to find another route when I realized, by the huge stadium lights in my eyes, that it was a DWI check. After selling *Responsible Alcohol Service* training for the NRA, I knew the *worst* thing you can do in that situation is back up.

I slowly moved forward. I was driving my parents' car. Recently, for Christmas, I had gotten my dad Purple Heart License plates (he has two purple Hearts from the Battle of the Bulge) and hoped that the cops might see that, smile, and wave me through. When I was front and center, a policeman put his head inside the car right in my face. He asked me if I had been drinking. "NO, SIR," I said. He asked me where I was coming from. I didn't want him to know I was coming from a wedding, so I improvised. Do you remember the episode in *Seinfeld* where Elaine is lying to some guy she does not want to date and tells him she is busy running an import-export company and does not have time to date him? He asks her what she imports, and I think she says bananas. He asks her what she exports, and I think she says toothpicks. It was classic.

So, here I am in a long, blue, beaded gown driving a champagne-colored Lexus on a Saturday night, and the cop asks, "Where are you coming from?" I replied, "The library." He said, "Where are you going?" I said, "The airport." He looked at me, smirked, and waved me through.

PHEW! I got to McLintocks. When I got out of the car, there was a Honda car key under my butt. I went to the pay phone in the back of the bar and called back to the Surf Club and asked them to connect me to the valet. I shared that there was an unknown key that had been left on the seat of my car. They asked around and then said it was one of the valet drivers and must have fallen out of her pants pocket. Could I drive back and give it to her? I told them, "NO WAY." But that I was at McLintocks in Pelham if she wanted to get it after work and if I was gone, I would leave the key with the bartender.

And Then...

Hours later, the female valet from The Surf Club walked into McLintocks. My friend and I used to sing the national anthem at Major League ballparks all over the country (nine in total) and we were standing on chairs singing the National Anthem to the entire bar, with everyone standing, cheering, and saluting us, just at that very moment. She must have thought she stepped into the BOZO Twilight Zone, but it was a night to remember for sure!

Soon after I moved to Chicago, my friend Annie Munana invited me to a party at her home. Annie worked at Northwestern Hospital at the time. I met a nice lady who worked with Annie and asked her what she did. She said she oversaw ID.

In different parts of the country, people refer to having someone check their driver's license in different terms. Some say I got carded, some say proofed, but where I come from, they said, *ID'd*. So, I replied, "So you actually make sure that the people who say they work at the hospital really work there when they arrive at Northwestern?" She looked at me, smiled indulgently, and said, "No actually, I run the Infectious Disease Department." I turned beet red, said, "I bet that pays way better," and snuck off into the kitchen!

And Then... I remembered that these crazy stories seem to be the fabric of my life! You're in good company. It is OK to be a BOZO!

It is OK to Be a BOZO!

Has there been a time in your life where you did something that was very embarrassing, and you thought you would never recover from it? Don't beat yourself up. None of us wakes up in the morning thinking, *I'm going to mess things up today!*

Just keep doing your best and don't be afraid to laugh at yourself. We are all only human!

I saw this sailboat in the Chicago Harbor when on an Absolutely Segway Tour. It reminded me of my Dad's word choice blunder when giving a speech while working for Union Carbide!

And Then...

Chapter Six

Planes, Trains, Automobiles, and Wrigley Field

In the mid '80s, I was heading on a Metro North train into New York City to meet up with some camp friends at McSorley's Ale House in lower Manhattan. A young, pretty, blonde Irish lady named Angela sat across from me on the train and I could tell she was very excited about something. We started chatting and she shared that she had just landed a job as a nanny in Pelham and was hoping to go out to celebrate in NYC with some friends, but they had all canceled on her. I said, "Why don't you come out with me and my friends tonight?" She said, "Really?" I said that I was meeting my great friends from my Catholic sports camp, and it would be a lot of fun and they were all very nice. She was itching to have a good time and could tell that I was friendly and said, "Sure." I then suggested that we have a little fun and *not* tell my friends that we just met on the train that evening. Instead, I proposed that we tell them that her dad was my dad's client, and we knew each other through our fathers. She said, "Okay."

Hours later, after many cab rides and bars and stories, my friends consistently asked Angela throughout the night how she knew the McCartneys. (We were probably seven people total.) We just kept making up work stories about our dads, story after story, and laughing. I forget where we were, but we were sitting at a round table in a corner at a restaurant or bar when Angela looked at me and said, "I can't keep this lie going any further. We have to tell them." My friends looked at me oddly after Angela said that, and I said, "We have to come clean. The truth is, Angela is not my father's client's daughter… We just met on the train tonight coming from Pelham into Grand Central Station." They all burst out laughing that we had been together all night and she hadn't broken her cover.

A year later, I sang at her wedding.

In early 1991, I was flying back to Chicago from a weekend in NY setting up my parents Surprise 40th wedding anniversary party at the New Rochelle Rowing Club to be held later that spring. Many people were involved in this deceptive hook of getting my folks to attend, including the Harrisons and Mom's friend Betty. Betty's husband had rowed for the New Rochelle club, so she invited my parents to a *fake* reunion. We had the caterers in red vests so they would look like valets out front for when my parents arrived. I thought Mom was going to have a heart attack when she came up the steps and everyone yelled, "Surprise!" She was initially upset that she had canceled her hair appointment that day, but once she entered the room, heard the piano player we'd hired from *One if by Land, Two if by Sea* in NYC, and saw all the people from their lives who had traveled from near and far, she didn't care. My brother Drew had put together a slideshow of their lives, and a good time was had by all.

But back to the flight months before… I got on the plane at LaGuardia heading home to O'Hare, and I had been assigned a window seat. I always like a window seat in case I want to take a nap; I can use the wall to rest my head. As I approached my aisle, I saw that there was already a woman sitting in my seat, sleeping against the wall. Part of me was angry, but part of me was jealous! I woke her up, much to her dismay, and said, "You are in my seat." She said she was hungover, and was hoping no one had been assigned to that seat. I said I was in the same boat and needed to sleep, so she moved to the middle seat. We slept most of the short hour and a half flight, but then began chatting right before we landed at O'Hare. Her name is Patty and she lived in Lincoln Park. As we were deplaning, I said I needed to get a cab to Wrigleyville, and she offered to share a cab since she lived nearby. A friendship was born and thirty years later, we are still friends! A few years after we met, I was at her wedding shower, and she has come to my Christmas party many times over the years. She and her husband Hank still live in Lincoln Park in a great place on Armitage. We had not seen each other in a while, so we got together in person last year before COVID-19 shut everything down.

There are great people all around us. We just must keep our eyes and heart open!

In or around 1999, I was at the last home Cubs game of the sea-

Planes, Trains, Automobiles, and Wrigley Field

son at Wrigley Field. I was with my buddies Allen Tait and Ken Meyer. Allen went to Bethany with me and met Ken at UW Madison in Grad School, which is how we got connected initially. As is the tradition, we were standing for the last out of the game because the Cubs were winning. I turned and saw two guys behind us sitting and said, "Hey, guys, are you going to stand up for the last out of the game? Where are you from anyway?"

They replied with cool accents, "New Zealand, mate!" I apologized and explained that we were heading over to Bernie's on Clark Street afterward. It was our go-to hangout after games. I invited our new Kiwi friends to join us. Their names were Terry and Shane, and they were roommates from Auckland. Hours later, we were dancing in the rain in front of Bernie's, and they told me they were staying in a youth hostel in a bad neighborhood on the west side. I had a spare bedroom with two beds and said, "You should check out of that place and spend the last few nights of your vacation in Chicago with me. You guys are great, and I trust you." They could not believe it!

I took them out and about to local spots for fun for the next few nights. They loved all my friends, and we had a blast. They just kept saying, "What can we ever do to repay you?" I replied that I was planning on going to the Olympics with my friend Susan from New York the following year in Sydney, and that maybe we could pop over to New Zealand after Australia on the way home and visit them. They said, "*For sure*! You can stay with *us*!"

Consequently, after our trip to Sydney for the Olympics, we flew to Auckland and spent about four nights with Terry and Shane. They were great. We went to a casino one night and I ended

And Then...

up winning $1,000 playing roulette, which was awesome. These winnings were particularly helpful, because at the time, I had just started a new job north of Chicago. Just prior to that, I had been working at a television/radio studio downtown for less than a year, where I met my buddy Joe Jamrosz, (loved by *all*!) I had only been at this firm for six months, and although my boss kept telling me that I was going to be great, she never really explained what it was that I was going to be great at. I felt a little lost. At one point, I had an assignment to sell private tents for a big golf tournament in the western suburbs. Due to my connections, I sold them out in two days. Now what? She and the rest of the folks in the small office were all nice, but when this other opportunity came along and a client asked me to consider an opportunity with them at their company in Highland Park, I jumped at it. It was more money, and I had clear direction and knew what my role would be. I needed more structure.

When I interviewed with the CEO, he offered me the job. I had to tell him I had a three-week vacation to Australia for the Olympics and then New Zealand planned for September 2000, and hoped it was not a problem. He graciously said not to worry about it. I was so appreciative that I spent $500 buying Olympic hats for everyone in the office and shipping them back to Highland Park from Sydney. My winnings in Auckland helped pay for the cost of those hats of appreciation! After all, what goes around should come around.

In June of 2019, I was taking a colleague named Alli, who had just moved to Chicago from the PRA Arizona office, to her first Cubs game on a Thursday night at Wrigley Field. They were playing the Colorado Rockies. I had our two tickets in the bleachers.

I told her to meet me in the outdoor area in the front of Murphy's Bleachers. I got there early to try to get seats and ordered a vodka with cranberry. It was a hot night, and two guys I did not know were sitting at a table with three chairs. I had my eyes fixed down the block in Sheffield looking for Alli to come walking up when one of the guys offered to let me sit with them. I gratefully accepted. They were in town on business from Kansas City and were excited about going to a game. One of the guys, Sean Devlin, was from Overland Park, Kansas, and we ended up chatting and buying each other drinks before Alli showed up. Sean shared that his brother Bobby and his father Brian were flying in from New Jersey and meeting him in town for the game on Friday afternoon and Saturday against the St. Louis Cardinals. Neither of them had been to a Cubs game before, and this was a big and always an action-packed weekend. I shared that my birthday was that Saturday and my husband and I were having a barbeque pregame, and he always cooks enough for an army. I invited Sean, his dad, and his brother to our place. We had a blast! Gary had ordered king crab legs to be flown in from Alaska because he knows how much I love them. A feast for everyone, including our new friends.

In 2016, our annual meeting was in New Orleans in late August. I love New Orleans and the PRA staff did not disappoint. It was

And Then...

an amazing few days of fun, education, and celebration. It was spectacular!

At that time, my colleague and friend Gabby Spanton, from Toronto, had been promoted from being a Global Sales Director (GSD) to being the Director of the Global Sales Team. My colleagues and I were blown away that she made sure that the GSDs were recognized in a special reception prior to the start of the annual meeting. It was one of the many highlights of my fifteen years with PRA. We were all so very happy to be specifically appreciated in a public forum. I think since Gabby knew how we felt, having walked in our shoes, she made it a non-negotiable part of the deal for her promotion. I will always love her for that, and for being a great person and friend.

On the opening night, the president of our PRA NOLA office, Jeff O'Hara, and his team organized a second line parade for us all from the Intercontinental Hotel (which was a wonderful host hotel!) to a private party at Bourbon Vieux. Though we had known our NOLA team organized this event regularly for our clients, it was an entirely different thing to be participating in it ourselves! We were all blown away. I loved every second of it. People videotaped us from the sidewalks, us throwing them beads and them throwing them back. News crews filming and just happy people everywhere. New Orleans is infectious when it comes to *fun*.

The meeting culminated at our annual awards dinner held at the WWII Museum. I had recently purchased a brick in honor of my father's service in the Battle of the Bulge. I snuck out of our event to go give a quick hello to Dad at the bottom of the stairs

Planes, Trains, Automobiles, and Wrigley Field in the Campaign of Courage Hall.

On the Friday of Labor Day weekend, I had a flight back from NOLA to Chicago and was taking a client of mine, Karen, to the Cubs game that afternoon. They were playing the San Francisco Giants. I had asked her to join me, pregame, for lunch at the Audi Club inside the ballpark.

At the gate at the Louis Armstrong New Orleans International Airport, I sauntered over to a coffee bar. There was a kid there who was tall and wearing an orange San Francisco Giants shirt. He looked sixteen but I think later I discovered he was twelve. While waiting for my coffee, I asked him if he was going to the game at Wrigley that afternoon. He shared that in fact he was, with his dad. Neither of them had ever been to Wrigley or, in fact, Chicago before. Because it is second nature to me, I pulled out my business card and said if they needed anything while they were in town, they could call me for help. I wrote down a few places I thought he and his dad might enjoy for lunch pregame in Wrigleyville. The father's name was Cole, and the son was Casey. Cole came out of the men's room and gave me the once over like, "What is that lady doing talking to my young son?" I introduced myself immediately and explained that I had made some recommendations for lunch pre-game to his son, Casey.

Later, on the plane, they were just four rows in front of me. I saw them and thought, if it is their first trip to Chicago and Wrigley, they would probably love to go to the Audi Club for lunch. I invited the father and son to join us at the club. They seemed thrilled. I told Cole to text me ahead of time, to make sure I was at Wrigley, and though he forgot, it still turned out okay. I told him

And Then...

to ask for Bea at security for the Audi Club when he got there.

When I arrived, Bea said, "Your friends from New Orleans are here!" I was a bit surprised, but happy they'd gotten in with no problems. I found them at a four top in the middle of the room. I sat down with them, and we chatted for a bit until Karen showed up. Turns out both Karen and Cole went to the University of Houston, so they were talking about U of H, courses, teams, teachers, etc. Cole insisted on buying us a thank you drink... And then...

Tom Ricketts, owner of the Cubs, walked in. He was passing our table when I popped up to say hello. Though I doubt he really remembered the several times he had met me in the past (including at my bachelorette party in the bleachers), with all the people he meets daily, he was still very congenial.

I said, "I'd like to introduce you to some friends I met on the flight from New Orleans today who flew in for the Cubs game. It's their first trip to Chicago." He shook both their hands and said it was a pleasure to meet them. When Tom walked away, Cole looked at Casey and said, "Son, we will remember this day for the rest of our lives!"

I had to think when the Cubs won the World Series in Cleveland two months later, and they kept showing Tom Ricketts holding the MLB Commissioner's Championship trophy on TV, that somewhere Cole was sitting with some friends, drinking beer in New Orleans saying, "We had lunch with that guy!"

And Then... I was reminded...

Planes, Trains, Automobiles, and Wrigley Field

We *all* start off as strangers! Every day we never know what lies ahead. We can stay back or jump in and engage. Helping new people in your life can be a game changer and usually for the better.

You might want to take the earbuds out, lift your head from your phone screen, and have a conversation with the people who are around you in the moment.

June of 2019 at Wrigley Field with Kathleen Wood, Tyler Barros, Sean, Brian, and Bobby Devlin (who we just met that weekend), Gary and me.

Chapter Seven

Making People Feel Worthy

*"People will forget what you said,
people will forget what you did,
but people will never forget how you made them feel."*

-Maya Angelou

My favorite teacher ever was Si Miller from seventh grade Social Studies at Pelham Junior High School. He not only taught my four siblings, but he was the JV Football Coach in Pelham. He coached all my brothers, and they thought he was the best coach they ever had. He was part of the inspiration behind my brother Ray becoming a football coach. Ray has had a successful college football coaching career at many schools including Ball State, Bowling Green, Ohio University, Wittenberg University, Wake Forest, Army, and now Davidson in North Carolina.

Si was "THE MAN." Many of my friends who played football for him said that they would run through a brick wall for Coach Miller. He treated everyone with respect and always made you laugh, often at yourself. He just had "IT" and not just as a teacher and a coach but as a human being.

When he was still in Michigan (before he moved to NY), he had a coaching interview. Though he had a strong knowledge of foot-

Making People Feel Worthy

ball and basketball, he would be paid more money if he coached tennis as well. So, when they asked him if he could coach tennis too, he said, "Sure," even though he had never picked up a tennis racquet in his life. He took the job and bought a book on how to play tennis, and in typical Si Miller fashion, his tennis team went on to win the district championship!

Mom and Dad adored Si from the moment they met him after he moved to New York. He and his awesome wife Helen were guests at our home for dinner on several occasions.

Not only did we look forward to attending Mr. Miller's Social Studies class every day because he made learning fun, but he would always go out of his way to make his students feel good. Seventh grade was the first year the four elementary schools came together. We did not already know all the kids in our classes. It was a little different from the comfort experienced being with the same kids we'd known since kindergarten. One day, Mr. Miller came into class, took his tie, and threw it over his shoulder, took his pointer, and swept it across the room in his hand and said, "Did anyone here see McCartney's brother on the football field this weekend? He was brilliant!" Since Ray is three years older than I am, it must have been a play that he made on the JV team. I cannot remember which play it was exactly, but I remember how special Mr. Miller made me feel in that moment. That *moment* was forty-seven years ago, and I still remember blushing with pride. We all can create a *moment* like that for someone every day if we try.

We stayed in touch and continued to visit them in Michigan when they returned. I was so grateful that Helen and Si drove

And Then...

to Pelham for our wedding in 2012. He gave a great toast at the rehearsal dinner to Gary, and my whole family, at the NYAC.

Unfortunately, Si died in October 2016, during the Cubs World Series run. The world lost such a wonderful person, such a wonderful soul, mentor, father, grandfather, brother, husband, and friend. I loved this man so much. Si, like my father, was the kind of person who could make you smile just by walking through a door. Your heart felt it. I have always been attracted to warmth and humor!

On Wednesday, Nov 8, 1989, I flew from LaGuardia to Midway Airport in Chicago to interview for some jobs in the hospitality industry. At the time I had been working in NYC for a hotel company as a National Sales Manager. I took an October vacation to be a tour guide in Russia and visited Moscow, Leningrad, Kiev, Kishinev, and Lvov. Though educational and enlightening, on the flight home, when they announced that we were out of Russian airspace, the whole plane applauded. Upon landing at Kennedy airport from Moscow, I think I French-kissed the ground (or thought about it!). After just having such an amazing experience and seeing so much, I decided to make a change in my life. I decided to move from Pelham and explore other options, other cities.

I narrowed down new possible locations to live...between Boston, where I had a lot of friends, and Chicago, where I had a lot of brothers. I flew to Chicago first and landed at Midway. I rented

Making People Feel Worthy

a car and was driving north on Lake Shore Drive. Just after the bend in the road near McCormick Place where you see Soldier Field and the Chicago Skyline at the same time, I remember thinking, *I could live in this city!* I stayed at my brother's house in Uptown and had a full docket of hotel sales interviews lined up for the next day.

My first interview was at the iconic Drake Hotel. I met their Director of Sales (DOS), Lee Pomeranz, in the Palm Court just left of the main lobby, where they typically serve high tea. It is a refined 1920s hotel with classic rooms and lake views that are often shown in movies of Chicago.

I had called Lee about an interview, and he said he would meet with me. He was a smaller guy, well dressed, with a firm handshake and an easy smile. He had a nice, comfortable way about him. At the end of our conversation, he said, "I wish that I had a sales position for you because I know you are going to be a star in Chicago."

I was twenty-eight years old. How do you think that made me feel? Like a million bucks, that's how!

I took a job at the Knickerbocker Hotel as their Corporate Sales Manager. My KCH (Knickerbocker Chicago Hotel) interview was my last of the day and I had so much coffee in me I was speaking fast, and I already speak fast. They paid for my moving expenses, gave me a nice raise, and put me up at the hotel until I could find my own apartment. WOW! I canceled my Boston interviews for the next week. I had found my new home in Chicago.

And Then… I remembered that kindness is always remembered.

And Then...

Making others feel valued builds connection.

Who has gone out of their way to make you feel special? It can be in a family situation or a work situation. It's always nice to be around people who appreciate you for being you.

"Be yourself. Everyone else is already taken!" ~Oscar Wilde

Si Miller, (center in black) a beloved PMHS coach and teacher, playing hockey with his sons in Michigan. From left to right: Tom, Joe, Si, Jack and Daniel Miller.

The Kindness of Strangers

With my pal Heather McLeod Greacen.

Chapter Eight

The Kindness of Strangers

When I was in fourth grade, Mike and Joan Greco and their family moved to Pelham from Pelham Bay in the Bronx. They had five kids: John, Michele, Maryann, Carolann, and Michael. Michele was in my class at Prospect Hill Elementary School. She was shy initially, but we were both big sports fans. She was always very nice, and we became friends. She shared this story with me years ago and it has always stuck with me. Stuck in my heart.

One night, right before Christmas, over thirty-five years ago, her dad had taken the family in their big Lincoln Town Car to his favorite restaurant in the Bronx, Joe Nina's. On the way back to Pelham, they noticed a car with Vermont license plates broken down on the side of the road. Her father pulled over to see if anyone needed help. Inside the car was a couple with their two small children. They were driving from their home in Vermont to spend Christmas with their family on Long Island. Michele remembers that the husband was a chef at a private boys' school. When Mr. Greco could not get the car started either, he suggested that they all pile into their large car to go to their house on Priory Lane, and they did. Once there, Mrs. Greco fed them and, knowing how out of sorts the children must have felt, gave some of the wrapped gifts they had for their own children under the tree to these young kids from Vermont. The mother pulled her children over and said, "Remember how mommy always tells you about the spirit of Christmas? Well, that is what these nice people are doing for us right now." Then Mr. Greco suggested they leave their car keys, and he would have his mechanic tow their car in the morning and fix whatever was wrong. In the meantime, he said, "You can take my wife's car and drive out to be with your family for the holidays on Long Island. When you are done, you can stop back here in Pelham and we will switch back cars and you can continue your way home to Vermont."

Michele said after they left, her mother jokingly said, "Say goodbye to the car, kids!" All went as planned. Michele remembers that they came back with a huge tray of cookies for everyone and an abundance of *gratitude* for saving Christmas.

Any Catholic Pelham people reading this probably know Father Michael Greco. He is the youngest in this great family, who grew up to be a beloved priest in his hometown parish. He learned early on what it means to be a Christian. He had a great example in his parents!

On Monday, July 22, 2019, I got early morning texts from my sister and my mom's wonderful neighbor, Jim Donahoe. They both said that Mom had fallen in the bathroom and was bleeding from her mouth. Mary took a car service to Pelham from NYC and called the dentist Mom had seen recently, thinking it was a dental issue. When the dentist opened that morning, Mary and

And Then...

Mom were the first ones in the door. The dentist said that the bleeding had nothing to do with any dental issues. Mary went back to Mom's and took a nap with Mom in her bed. When Mom got up to go to the bathroom, thank goodness, Mary walked beside her. She caught her when she fainted. Mary immediately called an ambulance.

That day, I had a big site inspection at the Museum of Science and Industry just south of downtown Chicago. It was for a huge association program and there were probably 100 people at the meeting. When I arrived home, my sister texted me that she was getting into an ambulance with Mom. Two minutes later, she texted me again that Mom wanted me to come home. I booked my flight on American Airlines in minutes and told her I was on the 4:30 flight. Jim Donahoe, our trusted neighbor, said he would pick me up at the other end.

There were huge storms that day and night, and everything was shutting down. Flights into New York were getting canceled, and while I was in a cab to O'Hare, they canceled mine. I went to the Admirals Club and asked them to get me on anything they could to New York. Not knowing what was going on with Mom, I was petrified that she might die that night, and I needed to get home to see her. Literally, I was offering cash to people online to board, but everyone just looked at me like I was weird. I did not care. Still, no one offered to give me their seat, which I understood. Everyone has stuff going on in their own lives. They did not know me from a hole in the wall. Still, I just kept praying something good would happen.

I returned in tears to the Admirals Club and approached a woman named Lynn at the far-right kiosk. She saw me in tears and offered to help me. She got on her computer and asked, "Can you go to Newark?" I replied it was not ideal but would go with whatever would get me to the East Coast. She then said, "How about White Plains?" I told her that would be perfect. She got me listed on standby for the last flight out, which was leaving soon. She said I would have to hurry to make it to the L terminal. With only a small carry-on, I dashed off, looking for the gate with my small blue wheelie flying behind me.

Many people were sitting around the gate, hoping to get on this last plane. Though I visited the counter, they told me they would call my name if I got on. I met a nice man who offered to drive me to the hospital if I needed help on the other side, *if* he made the flight. I saw a woman wandering around and thought, *please be going to Kentucky or someplace else*. But she was on the plane, too. With each late arrival boarding, my hopes sank.

Finally, I heard "Margie McCartney" and could not believe it. I got to the counter and there was a blonde woman standing in front of the gate near the ticket scanner. The man scanned my ticket, and I was in seat 8A. I said, "Pretty good seat for stand by!" The blonde lady said, "That was my seat." I said, "You decided not to go to NY tonight? Lucky me!" She replied that she just decided to stay in Chicago. Though she was not in a flight attendant uniform, as I walked down the ramp to the plane, I thought to myself that Lynn at the Admirals Club probably wrote something beautiful and emotional in the note section of my ticket and that this woman gave up her seat so I could get home to be with my mom. Another angel in my life.

And Then...

Our neighbor Jim picked me up at Westchester Airport in White Plains in the pouring rain and shared that my mom had taken a turn for the worse. I did not even know what was going on and was crazy with worry.

When I got to the hospital, Mom's face was bruised from her fall. She did not look great and was hooked up to machines. My sister, our friend Sallie, and my cousin Meg were there, and a priest from OLPH had already given my mother last rights. Mary and I spent the night with her in the room. In the middle of the night, Mom needed to go to the bathroom. Mary went to find a nurse and a bed pan, and Mom started saying, "Why is it taking so long?" over and over. I replied that Mary would be back soon with the bed pan. She asked, "Why is it taking so long to *die*?" I lost it and began sobbing.

At 6:30 the next morning, I was standing beside Mom's bed and Mary was standing at her feet. Mom was sitting up and suddenly started vomiting blood. It was very scary and looked like she had slugs in her blood. It was out of a movie. I was so scared; Mary was so scared; and Mom was so scared. I raced to get assistance, and when the nurses asked one of the assistants to help clean up my mom, he said something negative and nasty, and I told him he might want to get another job. The door was open, and my mom might have heard him.

The next morning was Tuesday the 23rd. We signed the DNR. It all seemed so surreal to me. How could this be happening?

Five transfusions later, by Wednesday, she was looking at the newspaper again. By Thursday, she was walking the halls with the Physical Therapist, and by Friday, we were taking her home. So grateful were we!

On my next trip through O'Hare, I went back to the Admirals Club to look for Lynn, but she was not there. I left her a box of chocolates and a note of thanks telling her how much her act of kindness meant to me. My mom was on the mend, and I got to be there for a very scary night to hold her hand. I remember when Lynn was trying to help me get on that plane, another Admirals Club greeter said, "What are you doing?" and she said, "I am being naughty, but I don't care!"

I so appreciate when people know when to push the limits and be a good human being first! Screw the rules!

In the autumn of 1981, I went to school for a semester at Wagner College, in Bregenz, Austria. The summer before, Mom and Dad said if they were paying for me to go to school in Europe, I could not go back to camp to make $500 for the summer being a camp counselor. So, I got a job being a cocktail waitress at the New York Athletic Club on Traverse Isle about a mile from my parent's house on Shore Road. I made $2500 for the summer and drove up to Livingston Manor in the Catskills every day off I had to be with my camp friends, especially Mooie, who was the Athletic Director that summer. Debby Germann was the Head Counselor that year. Her folks were legendary camp leaders for years before I even went there. She and her sister Kathe were my counselors when I was a camper and were very popular.

And Then...

In Bregenz, Austria, we had school Tuesday through Thursday and were on a train for another country many Thursday nights. I made a solo trip to Zurich because I wanted to buy a Swiss Army Knife and I wanted to get it in Switzerland. I had made a reservation at a Youth Hostel in Zurich over the phone. They were very clear that you *had to arrive* by 10 p.m. Even a *minute* later and they would not let you in. Well, long train ride, do not speak the language, not familiar with the area. I got a bit turned around.

I got off the train and made my way as best I could to the hostel, but the door was locked. I could see the reflection of a TV in the upstairs window and started throwing snowballs at the window, hoping to get someone's attention so they would come down and let me in. No one came down to open the door. No one even looked out the window.

I looked at my watch and realized it was 10:03. At that point, I cried, having no idea what I would do next. An elderly couple walked by and saw me crying. My German is not great, other than hello, goodbye, it is nice to meet you, may I have a beer, and where is the bathroom? They spoke little to no English. However, they knew I was upset and gestured to have me walk with them. This was all in sign language, mind you. They were very nice, and I knew no one was going to let me into the youth hostel. Going with this couple felt like being with my grandparents. I certainly felt safer than standing outside in the snow, in the dark, so I followed them. They ended up taking me to their home and giving me their daughter's room. She was older and had already moved out. The next morning, they made me breakfast and gave me a map of their town. They wrote down the name and address of a good store to buy a Swiss army knife. All this was basically done playing charades. No wonder it has become a game I love as an adult. It got me through a lot of jams over the years. I did keep in touch with Mr. and Mrs. Werner Hanggi from Mozart Strasse 3 in Luzern for several years. I still have a photo of them in my scrapbook, and they remind me how important the kindness of strangers has been in my life.

Later that same semester, a guy named Mark from Minnesota—who lived with my friend Hopper—and I decided to get up early one Friday morning and take a bus down to ski at Lech Zurs in Arlberg. The Arlberg comprises 350 kilometers of ski runs and is the largest connected ski area in Austria and the fifth largest in the world. We had a great day, and the mountains offered all sorts of various runs from easy to hard. We were both pretty good skiers, but I prefer the blue runs to the black, as does my back side!

Toward the end of the day in Lech, we found out that there had been a big avalanche and all the roads out of town were closed. We had no credit cards and no cell phones back then. We were nineteen. I do not even think we had debit cards to get cash in those days. We wandered the streets looking to find a hotel or motel that might be able to put us up for a night or so until the roads opened. For hours, we wandered around and asked everywhere we could think of and were told *no*! We had many doors closed in our faces.

And Then... we met our guardian angel.

We saw a woman sweeping in front of a sign that read: Haus Johanna. The proprietors were named Christine and Louis, and

And Then...

they could not have been nicer or more generous and understanding. We explained our predicament, and she offered to put us up until we could leave the area post-avalanche and get back to school. She even let us eat meals in the kitchen with her family. We said we could send her a check when we returned to Bregenz. Showers were extra money that we did not have, and we could not afford. Mark and I played cards and watched some TV (the little we could understand) to pass the time. I remember Christine said to us, "I only hope that if my daughter were ever in America, someone would do the same thing for her." I have never forgotten that and try to always pay it forward.

As it turned out, her daughter Johanna lived up the street from me in Bregenz, so when we got back, we paid her the remaining balance in Schillings and gave her a Christmas poinsettia for her parents, along with a heartfelt thank you card. My mom asked for her address so that she could also thank her. I will never forget that experience and to this day, if I see someone looking lost, I always try to help them.

Back in early 2000, I was working in downtown Chicago and went to the downtown post office to buy stamps on my way to the Chase cash machine on Michigan Avenue. I overheard two guys trying to mail their laundry back to their mom in Australia. It looked like a big ball rolled up in tape. Once I heard their accents, I knew they were Aussies. Turns out they were brothers from Adelaide, Australia. At the time, I was getting excited about returning to Australia later that year for the Olympics. I introduced myself to the brothers, Roger and Tim. They were young and funny and had just arrived in Chicago by train from NY. They really had no idea what to do but had heard great things about the Windy City. I gave them my business card and told them to call me if they needed anything.

At the time, I was working for a network in marketing downtown. After meeting them in the post office, I was walking to the bank and decided to check my Blackhawks schedule in my purse. The Hawks were home that night. While walking back to work, I ended up passing the Aussies again by chance on the street, just as it started to snow. Remembering how kind Christine and Louis from Haus Johanna had been to me, I wanted to pay it forward. I asked them if they wanted to go to a hockey game that night. They said, "Sure!" Later after work, I picked them up at their hotel in my car, and off we went to The United Center. A great time was had by all. I am sure they still root for the Hawks until this day. The next night, since I had some leftover spaghetti and meatballs from a dinner party I had recently hosted, I invited them to my home for dinner. While there, I suggested that they use my phone to call their mother, so she would know they were okay. Roger told his mom, "We met this crazy lady, and she is taking great care of us." They put their mom, June Adams, on the phone, and she thanked me for watching after her boys, which was my pleasure.

Later that year, when Susan Keary and I left Sydney after the Olympics, we went to visit some friends of hers in Melbourne. Great people, great family, and they were so good to us. They even took us to their beach house in Sorrento for a night or two. When we returned to Melbourne, June and her husband Brian

And Then...

from Adelaide, along with their sons Tim and Roger, who were back from their American adventure, came to visit. They rented a car and drove nine hours from Adelaide to Melbourne to meet Susan and me and say thank you in person. Australia is one of my favorite countries, and I have visited it four times. They love Americans, they speak English, and they love to have fun. A trifecta!

Several years later, Roger and his then girlfriend Lisa Briggs came together to visit me in Chicago. I took them to a Cubs rooftop for their first American baseball game. When they got married on Key Bridge in Central Park in New York City several years later, they asked me to be their witness. The year before, when my Chicago friends, Jimmy and Amy Clark, told me that they were planning to go to Australia for their honeymoon, I suggested that they connect with Roger and Lisa, which they did. No surprise, the Clarks too became their friends and joined us in Central Park for the wedding as well. Lisa looked stunning in a red satin dress with a beautiful white head scarf. She looked like Audrey Hepburn.

On June 1, 2005, just days after returning from New York and seeing my dad in the hospital over Memorial Day weekend battling cancer for the fifth time, my cell phone rang at my desk in Chicago. It was my oldest brother, John, saying Dad did not have much longer to live and to get home ASAP. This was a call I knew would come one day and over the years, when I interviewed for a job, I would think, if I got a call to get home right away, would someone here help me? Fortunately, a coworker drove me to the airport and let me stop home to put some things in a bag for the trip. I grabbed one of my favorite photos of my father and me. I sat in seat 3F of an American flight, squeezing the picture frame, crying the whole trip. The middle seat was empty, and a woman was sitting in 3D. At one point, she just reached over and held my hand. I looked at her through my tears and said that I was hoping to get home in time to say goodbye to my father, who was dying and whom I worshiped. She said she knew it was something bad. Her name was Julie.

We chatted and it turned out that she was a Marketing Manager for Heineken Beer in White Plains. I told her my dad/brothers/family loved to drink beer, and Heineken was a favorite. She asked me for my mom's address in Pelham, and I gave it to her. The next day, my father died on my parents' fifty-fourth wedding anniversary. When we got home from the hospital, low and behold, there was a case of Heineken Beer on my mom's front stoop with a note from Julie at Heineken. I had her business card and a few months later, Mom and I took her to lunch to say thank you in person.

After spending half of 2005 and half of 2006 in Pelham with my mom, I moved back to Chicago. But the following July 2007, I put together a sales mission to NY and New England. Several salespeople from PRA, around the country, came and stayed at my mom's house with me in Pelham, while we saw clients in the area. Then we saw some customers in Connecticut and drove

And Then…

up to Boston. There was an MPI (Meeting Professionals International) Boat Cruise on our first night and we all had signed up to attend. It was a beautiful, big, new boat and a perfect night for a sunset cruise in the Boston Harbor.

During most industry events, they have an auction as a fundraiser, and this was no exception. A place that I had always wanted to visit was Mirror Lake Inn, in Lake Placid, NY. One of the packages for the auction was a weekend at this hotel, including breakfast for two each morning. I bid on it immediately. It is not uncommon for another person to want the same thing you want in an auction, and a woman kept coming over after each of my entries and adding her name and number on top of mine with another, higher bid. Though I do not remember her name, I learned she was in the printing industry. I was determined to win a trip to this great hotel and made sure that when the time came that they ended the auction, that my name and bid was the last entry.

When they announced that I had won the weekend at the Mirror Lake Inn, printer lady went *crazy* yelling that she should have won it. Not sure how she came up with that, but she made such a fuss that I went up to the MPI organizers of the group, whose mouths were dropped open because this lady was making such a scene, and said, "Just give it to her." You could see that they were not happy about dealing with this woman. Though I really wanted it, it seemed like an easier fix to just shut her up and give her what she wanted.

A few minutes later, a nice young man who had been watching this situation unfold walked up to me and handed me his business card. His name was Christopher Jarvis, and he was and still is the Director of Rooms at the Mirror Lake Inn Resort and Spa in Lake Placid. He said, "I saw what you just did. Sorry about that. You have my card now, so you just let me know when you want to come up and I will take care of you." We went up over New Year's Eve a year later, and he took *awesome* care of us!

Sometimes when you lose, you really win!

Habtamu, My Ethiopian Hero

In September 2017, I got very sick after a wonderful week in Greece, where I ate different kinds of food than I usually do at home and surely drank more wine than usual with friends. On the way home from Greece, I stopped to visit my friend Salvatore and his family in Rome. My niece Maddy flew in from New York to meet me in Rome. We had a great time, though as I was preparing to leave Rome, I sensed I had caught some bug and felt very ill.

The night before I was to fly back to the USA, Salvatore's wife, Valentina, who is a nurse, told my friend Salvatore to take me to the emergency room. I was in so much pain and could not keep anything down. I ended up at the Gemelli University Hospital, which is the Pope's hospital, and they did tons of tests on me. After giving me a sonogram, the nurse said to me, "Did you know you have a *huge* gallstone!" I was curious to know why nothing was staying down. Nothing wanted to stay in my body! They gave me some prescriptions to fill. They told me to try to

And Then...

just eat chicken and rice for a few days. I texted my husband the update in the middle of the night, Chicago time. The next morning at the Rome-Fiumicino International airport, I hit the ladies' room about three times before my flight, petrified to be so sick crossing the ocean. I figured I would spend most of the flight in the bathroom. However, I was surprisingly fine the whole flight, which was an unexpected gift. As usual, I read a book and watched lots of movies. Perfect.

Finally, I landed, cleared customs, and got in a blue taxi at the international terminal of O'Hare. Before long, I had to ask my driver to stop for me to get sick. He was so kind and nice to me. *Four* more times I had to ask him to stop. Can you imagine? Most drivers anywhere would be like, "Hey, lady, get out of my cab! Time is money!"

At one point I was in so much pain that I was lying down in the back of the cab crying and telling him that I wanted to die. The driver said, "I have been a cab driver for twelve years and I have never seen anyone so sick before!" I kept saying how sorry I was, and when he got to my apartment building on the corner of Irving Park and Pine Grove Ave, he offered to help take my luggage upstairs for me. He was so kind. I asked him how much the fare was, and he said $50. I gave him $80 in cash and did not even get a receipt. I did not know his name. My head was spinning, and I could barely function. I did remember when he took my luggage out that there was a child's seat in the back of his car. I knew he was a father. Gary had been so thoughtful to leave work early and go home to make me chicken and rice, but I could not eat a thing. My husband wanted to take me directly to the emergency room as soon as I walked through the door, but I said that I just needed to sleep, and we would go in the morning.

The next day we went to the Northwestern Clinic on Belmont, and they gave me a thorough once over. Naturally, I gave them all the paperwork from the emergency room in Rome, but that was not much help as it was all in Italian! I shared that the doctor in Rome had said I had a gallstone. They felt around the right side of my stomach area and asked me, "Does this hurt?" over and over. Nothing did, but they said if it ever did, I should go to the emergency room right away. He was 99 percent sure that I had a traveler's bug and that it would go away in a week. He gave me antibiotics…always seems to do the trick.

I lost ten pounds in a week, but not the way you would want to for sure. Once I had recuperated, I knew I had to find the driver to let him know how much I appreciated his kindness. I knew his skin was black and that he was from Ethiopia, and he drove a blue cab. I knew he was the nicest person I could possibly have had driving me home in my condition. I had no idea how I could find him, but knew I had to thank him again somehow. Determined, I reached out to none other than my dear friend Ken. Ken said it was great that it was a blue cab and not a yellow one, as there were about 7500 yellow cabs but only about 2500 blue ones at the time. Within a week, Ken sent me the contact information for the driver including his photo, home address, and phone number.

I immediately got out some stationary and wrote a heartfelt thank you note and added a check for $50. The letter outlined to Habtamu that he had renewed my faith in mankind and that I appreciated his kindness to me at one of the *lowest* points in

And Then...

my life, more than he would ever know.

A few weeks later, I was flying to the annual IMEX trade show in Las Vegas, which is the biggest trade show in the hospitality industry, with hotels and convention bureaus and DMCs from around the world. My company was both exhibiting and entertaining clients and potential clients for future business. It is an awesome show.

Now that I had a new best friend cabdriver, Habtamu, I asked him if I could hire him to take me to Midway for my flight to Las Vegas. He did and we talked about our families and our friendship was sealed. Soon, Betty, Habtamu's wife, invited me over for lunch and I got to meet their son Yoel and their new baby girl Yovella.

On Easter Day, 2019, I invited them to the Cubs game, and we had a blast. They met me at our condo, and we walked the short eight minutes to Wrigley Field. It was their first Cubs game and I spoiled Yoel. I wanted to make sure that he got a full Cubs experience and bought him a Cubs jacket and hat. He is such a beautiful boy. Once when Habtamu was visiting his ill sister back in Ethiopia, Betty invited me over for lunch for a second time so I could meet her sister Etsy. (Habtamu told me we would also be fast friends). They made me traditional Ethiopian food, and I had no idea what it would be, but it was delicious. Betty even remembered that I have a delicate Irish tummy and did not make anything spicy. The Ethiopian custom is to eat with your hands. They have a form of bread that looks like an ace bandage that they use to pick up the various yummy dishes. It tastes great. I love this family. We facetimed Habtamu, in Ethiopia and his wife and sister showed me to him on their phone screen at their house, and he could not believe it as they had not mentioned to him that they had invited me over. They are the American Dream come to life.

Recently, Gary and I went over for dinner at their house in Rogers Park, and I got to meet Etsy's husband Mohamed. Terrific guy. They are all first-class people, and I am so grateful to have them in my life. Betty and Etsy and a friend of theirs came to our Christmas party in 2019 and were some of the last ones to leave. They were a huge hit, mingling with everyone. Beautiful people. Habtamu always says to me that when I retire, he is going to take me to Ethiopia to meet his family and friends there. I told him I plan to work till I am seventy, but I look forward to the trip!

And Then… I realized we can never know when we wake up one morning who we might meet that day. Someone touching our lives and changing it in a magnificent way!

Have you ever given up control to a stranger because you were so weak and had to trust someone you did not know?

Have you been the person to help a stranger when they were weak? It's a balance in this world but being kind to a stranger is always the best route to go.

And Then...

My cab driver, Habtamu Ambrelu's children now call me "Aunt Margie". This photo was taken weeks after we met when he drove me to fly to IMEX in Las Vegas.

Chapter Nine

Dealing with A**holes

Over the years, when I was younger, there was an obligation to attend several parties at an acquaintance's home. I was a social butterfly at six, and remember wandering around the parties, listening to bits and pieces of conversations with my Shirley Temple beverage. Networking came easily even then. The memory of this one specific day is so strong in my mind that I remember wearing a blue plaid dress my mom had made me. (The one in the family shot on the cover.)

Though I did not know what a racist was at that age, I knew the man of the house used words that were ugly, although I did not understand them.

On this day, while driving home from one of these parties, I sat up in the back seat of our wood-paneled station wagon and asked my dad, "Do you think people find the man of the house funny?" Dad said, "Why do you ask?" I replied that when he told a story, people around him were always laughing. (I was too young to distinguish the difference between genuine laughter and nervous, uncomfortable laughter.) Dad said, "Well, the next time he speaks, I want you to listen very carefully, because it's always about how he made a fool out of someone else."

And Then... I thought to myself that my dad was the smartest man I knew.

My buddy, Allen Tait, had a grad school friend I will just call Jay. He was getting married in March of 1993. They asked me if I could get a decent room rate for them and their guests at the Knickerbocker Hotel where I worked in the sales department. I checked with my boss, and we could offer them a $80 rate, which is a steal, even in the winter. Additionally, I got them the number two suite in the hotel, and I sent them some cheese trays, fruit plates, and champagne for the post party.

I was shocked that after our generosity, I did not get a thank you note from this couple. About two months after the wedding, the newlywed wife finally called me. I remember thinking, *Better late than never!* After some small talk and a brief thank you, she launched into getting her American Express bill and was surprised to see the $80 charge for the suite. She thought that was free. My mind was exploding and my hand holding the phone was shaking. If I could have leapt through the phone, I would have. How ungrateful can someone be? I emphasized that the suite she was charged $80 for was typically *very, very*, expensive and I reminded her that I personally paid to have amenities sent to the suite. She stumbled over her words and while still stuttering, I ended

And Then...

the call. Immediately, I called Allen, very upset. He could not believe that his friends whom I had helped because of my friendship with him could be so selfish and *cheap*! You know what they say: No good deed goes unpunished!

But, my classy friend, Allen, sent me flowers apologizing for his grad school friend and his new wife.

When my dear friend Susan Keary (met in Peltown taxi Susan) and I went to Australia for the Sydney Olympics in 2000, a friend who had been a waitress at a local spot we loved in Chicago called The Outpost was from Sydney and had hooked us up to stay with her friend Wayne. Wayne is a great guy. He had taken the day off work to greet us. Handsome and well dressed, he was a wonderful host. We were thrilled to have him give us the lay of the land at both his home and neighborhood. He also took the time to cook us a roast to have for late night after coming home from the Olympic games. Wow! This was even better than we could have expected. Before our time with him had ended, we had gone to several Olympic events with Wayne, had many wonderful nights out on the town in the Rocks area, and even climbed the Sydney Harbor Bridge, which was a thrill.

I had taken care of Susan's flight with my United frequent flier miles, so she reached out to a Sydney client of hers who offered to get us tickets to the opening ceremony of the Olympic games! For *free*! This was so exciting. We picked

Dealing with A**holes

them up but did not realize until we got to the stadium just how terrific the seats were. We sat in the second row of a VIP section twenty feet from where Kathy Freeman lit the torch! *Awesome.* Susan and I were both proudly wrapped in American Flags. As we were waiting for the games to begin, she went to buy us a few beers. Our seats were in the middle of the row, so if we went to the left or the right, we had to ask about ten people to stand. When she got back with the beers, she was visibly upset, and I asked what was wrong. She said that the man at the end of the row on the right had been rude. She asked him if she could get by and he said, "Only if you take your flag off." I had dreamed of going to (or being in) the Olympics my whole life. I wanted to go to the Olympics hosted outside the USA, where Americans were the minority. We were so proud to be wearing our American flags!

A few minutes later, I had to go to the ladies' room, so I decided to go left, avoiding the jerk at the end of the row. But, while sitting on the toilet, I got madder and madder and planned my speech. I returned from the right side and on cue, when I asked the man at the end of the row if I could get by, he replied, "Only if you take your flag off." I looked him straight in the eye and in my own Irish, New York way said, "My father fought with Patton against Hitler for me to have the honor of wearing this flag, and I have flown halfway around the world for this International Celebration of Humanity, so with no disrespect intended, please move your feet so I can get to my chair!" The whole section cheered for me, and better still, the guy's eight-year-old son just looked at him like "You are such a loser, Dad."

And Then... I learned that sometimes it feels good to quiet the bully!

We all must deal with difficult people on a regular basis. Try to keep smiling no matter what. Have any of you have ever had to stand up to a bully either for yourself or someone you care about? How did it make you feel?

It is a Small World After All!

As the babies in each of our respective families, my nephews, Evan, Sam and I certainly know how to embrace the small world stories that swirl around our busy lives!

Chapter Ten

It is a Small World After All!

My brother Drew met his best friend Andy Pitler working at American Hospital Supply in 1983. From there they went to Baxter Healthcare for years and became golf buddies and traveling companions. Andy had a buddy named Fish from Pittsburgh where he grew up. Drew knew Fish. They all would go on annual golf trips together.

One night, Drew and Fish were out in NYC, and Fish told my brother that he had just moved to Greenwich Ct. for a new job. Drew asked where and he said Dingletown Road. Drew said that our cousins, the Weihmans, lived on Dingletown Road. Turns out Fish was living in our cousin Ned's carriage house.

Fish shared that Ned, who like his father before him is a Chevalier de tastevin, often invited them over to taste some great wines. Ned would often do blind taste tests. We always enjoyed visiting with them as well!

In the mid 1980s, I invited my Bethany College buddy Jamie Trainor from Pittsburgh to the Jets vs. Steelers game at Mead-

It is a Small World After All!

owlands in New Jersey. Steelers fans are a breed unto their own and so passionate about their team, it is a blast to witness. At the time, Jamie was living in New Jersey.

I had been at our house in Peru, Vermont for a few days skiing at Bromley, but drove down to meet him for the game. I told him to meet me at a certain gate and that I would try to get there an hour before kickoff. Again, no cell phones back then. The traffic was bad, and I was delayed, plus it was snowing out so that did not help the situation. I was so late getting there that the game had already started. The whole time I was in the car I was angry at myself that I was so late. I had his ticket on me so it wasn't like he could meet me at the seats. I pulled in and parked and ran to the gate and there was my loyal friend, huddled against a pillar in the snow with the wind blowing in his face, all bundled up in his black and gold. I apologized profusely, feeling terrible. He shared that several people offered him tickets when they saw him huddled in the cold, but he said no, that he knew his friend Margie was coming. I am sure they did not think much of his friend at that moment!

Anyway, we got inside and settled into my sisters' season ticket seats, which were great seats in the lower level, close to the bar and bathroom. Soon we were a bit warmer with body heat all around and food and beverages. Jamie and I are always the type to speak to strangers, so with so many Steeler fans around us, he started chatting with the man sitting behind us in his black and gold wool hat. The guy asked Jamie where he was from in Pittsburgh. He said, "South Park Township." The man replied that he lived on Norrington. Jamie replied, "I grew up on Springvale." The man said he lived around the corner. Jamie asked, "What's

And Then...

your last name?" He replied, "Nish." Jamie laughed and said, "Oh my God, I used to mow your lawn as a kid!" 60,000 people in the stadium and Jamie runs into his old neighbor. Classic!

In August 1995, a friend from work at the National Restaurant Association Educational Foundation, Liz Shaw, told me that she was going to Africa on vacation for two months. She was heading over to visit a former exchange student, Marina, who had lived with her family. Liz would be traveling around the continent with Marina and her family. They would be celebrating her son Rory's fifth birthday during the adventure. Around the same time, another friend of mine from Northbrook, Illinois, Cassie Hillinger, told me that she was heading to Africa to go backpacking with a friend of hers from New Zealand. Cassie's family owned the Cypress Inn on Shermer Road in Northbrook and they had the best burgers and ambiance around.

Africa is a huge continent. It includes fifty-four countries, plus various archipelagos. I have never been but hope to go there one day!

A few months later, I ran into Liz. She walked up to me and said, "You are not going to believe this, but I just got back from my trip to Africa." She then shared the story about how they were in the middle of nowhere, having driven an hour down a bumpy dirt road to get to a lake area. There are not many lakes in Africa and my friend's kids wanted to swim. It was called Makuzi Beach in Malawi. They were staying at a hostel where you had electricity

It is a Small World After All!

for one hour at night. To shower, you had to get buckets from the lake. There were five people in the group and five other people sitting down for the evening meal that the proprietor had prepared. They were excited to celebrate Rory's fifth birthday and were shocked to learn that one of the gals in the group was also from Illinois! There they were sitting in a hut with a thatched roof having dinner when Liz told the Illinois gal that she worked for the Educational Foundation of the National Restaurant Association, and Cassie said, "Do you know my friend Margie McCartney?"

Maybe ten to fifteen years ago, I was attending an event in Colorado for the US Chamber of Commerce at the Broadmoor Resort. We had set up tours and excursions for the group, and the guys I knew from the Chamber invited me to join one of the tours. I decided to do the Jeep Tour. There were a variety of options, but that sounded like a winner to me. It was a beautiful day and I ended up in a Jeep with a woman and her daughter, also from Illinois. The mother's name was Kathy and she said they lived in Barrington, Illinois. I shared that I lived near Wrigley Field in Chicago. We were driving up a mountain on a dirt road, and I was telling her a story and mentioned Pelham. She said, "What did you just say?" I said, "The Pelham Train Station?" and she said, "OMG, are you referring to the Pelham in NY? I grew up in Pelham, NY!" I could not believe it. I asked what her maiden name was, and she said Stephens. I knew Kathy Stephens in high school, and she was a pretty girl and great athlete. This Kathy was attractive and looked athletic, but I had not seen Kathy Stephens since we were teenagers and now, we were in our fifties. I could not believe that this was the same person and yet, a minute later, I could clearly see it. We laughed and I said, "You lived on Ely Avenue near my friend Mary Jo Doherty." She said that they grew up playing with the Dohertys'. I had not spoken to Mary Jo in probably a year or so and decided it was a good time to make a call from the top of a mountain in Colorado to Mamaroneck, NY. Mary Jo answered on the second ring, and I said, "It's Margie. Hold on, I want you to talk to someone. It's a total blast from the past." They chatted for a while, and we laughed on a blue-sky day with the sun on our faces at the top of a mountain, feeling very lucky.

And then... I thought, what are the chances?

In 1989, just months before moving to Chicago, I was a tour guide in Russia. An industry friend in NYC named Janet had taken several groups to tour Russia over the years, and I told her that I would be interested in doing that too, so she set me up with an interview with General Tours, who put together the program. I ended up getting booked for the last trip out for the year in October.

The trip consisted of taking about fifty or so Americans to Moscow, Kiev, Kishinev, and Lvov.

We visited palaces and monuments and ate chicken Kiev in Kiev. I remember all the meat looked gray. The escalators to the sub-

It is a Small World After All!

ways went on *forever*, and they had armed guards with machine guns. What I had really hoped to bring home were three Russian hockey jerseys for my brothers for Christmas, but every time I was close to getting a deal done, someone would panic, thinking I was with the KGB, and the deal would fall through.

While we were on this trip to Russia in October 1989, there was an earthquake during the World Series in Candlestick Park in California. A nice young couple in our group who had been traveling the world lived in San Francisco. They had to cut their trip short to get home and check on the damage to their house. On our last night together, we had dinner at a hotel across from Red Square overlooking the Kremlin. I had written a song for my group to the tune of "Calendar Girl." (Camp girls always love to write songs!) I stood up in the corner of the restaurant and belted out the song using many names of the people in our tour group, so instead of, "January, starts the year off fine," it was more like "Nancy, she's our shopping Queen—in Moscow, if you know what I mean," etc. Afterward, a big Armenian man all dressed in black (think Odd Job from *Goldfinger*) with a black hat came up to me and said, "You are an American, aren't you?" I replied, "Yes, I am!" He knew about the earthquake at Candlestick Park and said, "Thank you for your help in Armenia. God Bless America; good luck in San Francisco."

If I had known, I had forgotten, that in 1988, there was a huge earthquake in Armenia, which is a former Soviet republic. 80 percent of Gyumri, Armenia's second largest city, was destroyed by the earthquake, leaving 400,000 people homeless. The US Government sent $10 million in aid and private US organizations sent an additional $40 million.

And Then...

He sent two bottles of top shelf champagne to our table! I still smile every time I think of that incredibly kind, appreciative gesture.

While flying to Boston for a convention in around 1996, a handsome young man was putting his bag in the overhead compartment when I noticed it said *General Tours* on the side of the bag. He sat down next to me, and I asked him about his relationship with General Tours, as that was the name of the company, I had been a guide for in Russia in 1989. He said that his dad owned the company! Wow, what are the chances. I think his dad owned several hospitality industry organizations if I remember correctly.

My seatmate's name was Tyler Noel, originally from Steven's Point, Wisconsin, and he too was in the hospitality industry. At the time, he worked for an international Convention & Visitors Bureau, but was not thrilled with his job. I was at the National Restaurant Association Educational Foundation at the time and knew we were hiring. He was smart, handsome, and funny, and I liked him right away. I got his resume to my boss, and he interviewed for a spot on our sales team in Chicago and got the job. I was thrilled.

When he showed me a photo of his family, I was immediately intrigued. He has a biological sister and then a Black brother adopted from Wisconsin and a Black sister adopted from Wisconsin and two adopted brothers from Korea. Though I never have met his parents, that photo immediately said to me that

It is a Small World After All!

these people are special.

He and his wife Tina live in Madison, Wisconsin, with their blended families.

Tyler supported Tina in earning her pilots license to make it easier to fly her kids back to their father for shared custody in Minnesota, instead of getting in the car and driving hours every other weekend. Last year, just a few weeks after Kobe Bryant's helicopter went down in LA, they were in the sky in their plane over the mountains in Colorado, and it was very foggy. Their instruments were going haywire, and they had to abort their flight! Gratefully, they parachuted to safety, and he got through to 911 with coordinates for the mountain patrol to find them. A miracle, for sure!

And then... I was reminded that life can change on a dime. Remember to always hug your friends and family, if for no other reason than you can! Celebrate just being alive!

What "small world" stories have changed your life?

Have you ever thought you were going to die and made a promise that, "If I live, I will never do xyz again," or, "I will make sure to always do xyz from now on?"

Who have you met in your life that made you think, "small world"? Who can you reach back out to and make the world even smaller?

My buddy Ken Meyer visiting my nephew Sam in Washington D.C.

Interviews

Next to me on the couch is Kelli Knoble Logue, behind her (blonde) is Darlene Kender Fornier and next to Darlene is Erika Garcia Hirt, whom I met when she worked at the Mexico Restaurant Association.

Chapter Eleven

Interviews

Years ago, soon after college, I headed into NYC for an interview at NBC. It was a low-level position as an assistant for a big wig. I made the mistake of only having one resume in my leather portfolio binder, which I thought, was spiffy. I took Metro North in from Pelham and probably had at least one cup of coffee in me. Though I would not recommend using the toilets at Grand Central Terminal, when you got to go, you got to go. Unfortunately, my only resume fell from my leather binder and into the toilet as I turned to flush it. I grabbed it but not until it had gotten wet. I felt like an idiot with the resume under the hand dryer in the Ladies Room, trying to get it to look OK before I headed to NBC in Rockefeller Center. I thought it was passable, but it did not really matter in the end. I walked into a huge office with lots of wood and many bookshelves and was greeted by the man who would be my boss. He was sooo handsome that I could not even breathe. He asked me my name, and I could not think of it. I think I said, "Isn't it on the resume?"

I did not get the job!

Interviews

Prior to moving to Chicago, I interviewed with a helicopter company in NYC. We did a lot of business with different helicopter companies setting up tours for our VIP groups. I showed up for the interview wearing the colors of their firm and handed the man my resume. He looked at my home address and said, "Pelham, I am moving to Pelham." He told me the house address, which was across from Prospect Hill Elementary School. I thought, this is great stuff.

Then he continued to ask questions, but he *never smiled once*. I just kept wondering, could I work for this guy every day if he did not even smile at our first meeting? I realized no, I could not. I had mentally checked out. My mom always said, "They need you more than you need them."

I did not want that job.

When I worked for Rick Connor at David Green Organization, we initially shared an assistant. I told him I needed my own and he agreed, so we put word out in the paper and industry publications about the opportunity.

One day, a woman maybe fifteen years older than I was (and I was probably in my mid-thirties at the time) came in for an interview. I noticed while she was in the waiting room, that she had four *very* large buttons on her blazer, two on each side. Upon further review, I realized that they were photos of Ringo Starr, John Lennon, George Harrison, and Paul McCartney.

And Then...

It occurred to me that she wanted me to know, since my last name is McCartney, that she was a Beatles Fan. I shook my head and invited her into my office. Halfway through the interview, she stood up, took her skirt, and twirled it 360 degrees around herself and sat back down. Stunned, I tried to keep a straight face, asked a few more generic questions, and ended the interview.

She did not get the job.

When the Knickerbocker Chicago Hotel was sold, I was asked if I wanted to stay with the company and leave the hotel. This ended up being a good call. At the time, ANVAN was looking for someone to represent all their Wisconsin properties, and that sounded like an adventure to me. I knew many of their salespeople at the hotels and many were my friends. I worked out of the Barclay Hotel on Superior St. in Chicago a few days a week, and then drove to Lake Geneva (about an hour and a half from Chicago) for a day or two as well. This was a good gig for about a year and a half. However, the commute sort of got to me. Though I enjoyed representing the Abbey, Lake Lawn Lodge, and Interlaken, it was just too much back and forth. I put out some feelers. A woman I knew from Chicago Women in Hospitality said that a lady she knew named Kathleen Wood was looking for someone to be the Association Sales Manager for the National Restaurant Association Educational Foundation downtown. The pay was right, and I was interested.

A few weeks later, Kathleen came to a luncheon that I was speak-

Interviews

ing at as President of Chicago Women in Hospitality, to meet me. She invited me to come interview for the job. In her office, she asked me if I knew how to use a computer. I replied, "If there is an on-off switch, I am your girl!" She laughed. She asked me many other questions and I had to interview with about five or six people in all. At the end of the interview, she asked me what I knew about the restaurant industry. I replied, "Well, I am the youngest of five from an Irish Catholic Family in New York, and we eat and drink a lot, very often in restaurants." She laughed again and I took that as a good sign. I got the job. I had tons to learn, but it was a great five-year adventure, with many of my greatest friendships made to last a lifetime. Honesty is the best policy!

About a year into my role at the NRA, I needed to hire an assistant who could help me with branching out to Mexico. We had our books translated into Spanish and wanted to get going with the Mexican Restaurant Association. My Spanish was limited to pretty much, "Donde esta el bano? and Cerveza por favor?" I went through a thick stack of resumes and narrowed it down to a few folks, but I already knew the gal I wanted to hire. I just needed to make sure that our personalities would jive.

Enter Kelli Knoble into my life. Kelli is a gorgeous, tall brunette with blue eyes who walked into our offices with a big smile and a firm handshake. Kelli was wearing dark palazzo pants and high heels and walking into the interview, she tripped and fell on her butt and made fun of herself. Pretty much everything I needed to

And Then...

know. While she was still on the floor, I said, "You start Monday." She laughed and said, "Don't you want to know anything else about me?" I said, "What's your favorite color?" She said, "Blue." I said, "Me too! You start Monday!"

We did sit down and chat more, but she not only ended up being one of the best hires of my life, but one of my best friends too. Recently, I drove up to her home in Winnetka to drop off flowers, chocolate, and wine for her fiftieth birthday. COVID-19 has us all celebrating on front stoops and lawns, but many friends in the area made the trip. One had put lawn signs up, and her friend Elena in California made a video of all of us toasting her! Kelli is da bomb!

Kelli got promoted and transferred into the meetings department. I had hoped she could snag me an invitation to a coveted Pebble Beach outing, but no such luck. So then, I had to find someone else wonderful to hire to take her place.

Enter Darlene Kender! Darlene showed up in the office with long blonde hair and a smile that could have landed her a toothpaste commercial. Her resume was fine, but again, I needed to make sure that we would mesh. I had three potential candidates. Darlene came first, and I just knew I was going to hire her but needed to give the next two candidates consideration too. She smiled all the time and laughed at my jokes, and I could tell she was a doer with great energy. After Darlene, a young man came to interview for the job and told me he and his wife would be moving from Iowa to Chicago. I asked him why the move and he started to cry and tell me about his marital problems. I really felt bad for the guy but thought to myself that surely, he had a friend he could share this pain with. Not the best interview strategy. After him, another woman came in who was nice, well dressed, and had a good resume, but I was already sold on Darlene.

Darlene is one of those people who could take a stick of gum, a paper clip, and a shoebox and build a plane. Therefore, she got the nickname MacGyver at the NRA Educational Foundation. One time when I was on a trip for work, a client was very anxious that I was going to be away because we were working on a project. I told her that Darlene Kender was the person who would take care of her while I was gone. I even mentioned that she was so capable of doing *anything* that we nicknamed her MacGyver. When I got back from my trip, I listened to my voice messages in the office, and I doubled over laughing. I called Darlene over to my cubical and played the message for her from this female client. She said, "Margie, I called while you were out and there is no MacGyver who works at the NRA!" Priceless!

Kelli Knoble Logue and I went to Darlene Kender Fournier's house in November for her fiftieth birthday as well, with signs and balloons, and we beeped our horns so her neighbors would know how much she is loved.

And Then... I realized how important it is to trust your instincts. Have you ever hired someone just knowing you would be lifelong friends?

Have you ever made a mistake and hired someone you thought was going to be great and they ended up being a nightmare?

Trust your instincts and you will usually not be disappointed.

And Then...

Kelli and I surprising Darlene on her birthday during COVID-19.

Golf

At a recent golf outing with Will Corkery, Bobby Logue and David Goetz.

Chapter Twelve

Golf and the People We Meet On the Course of Life

Growing up, one of my favorite sounds was the clickety clackity noise of golf spikes on the sidewalk. Both my parents were golfers, and all three of my brothers played golf and caddied around Westchester County. I did not start to play golf until I was thirty-two, which in retrospect is a shame. I wish I had started when I was five or so. I would be much better now, although I did shoot a hole in one once! I can hold my own but look forward to the day I retire (no time soon) and can play as often as I like!

When I decided to try out golf, I bought a set of PINGs that I still use today. I was addicted right out of the gate. In 2005, I participated in a golf outing. My dad had been battling cancer for a while. My plan was to move back to New York to help take care of Dad for a year, or for the time he had left. Unfortunately, God took him faster than we expected, and he died two days after I resigned from my job in Chicago. Still, I decided to stay with Mom for a year in Pelham. I was invited to play by my industry friend Dawn Penfold, in a foursome for the New Jersey MPI golf outing. I was thrilled to be participating. I needed to find a valid client who played golf to be my partner. Finally, I found a client who also golfed and was able to invite him to be my guest. He

Golf

accepted. We will just call him Joe Blow.

When I arrived the day of the outing in New Jersey, they had a room full of sponsors. They asked everyone to visit this vendor display before teeing off. My company often sponsored events, so I understood the importance of making sure to shake everyone's hand, talk to them about possible opportunities, take their card and leave yours behind.

While making sure I visited every booth, I saw a sign with the Ferris wheel from Chicago's Navy Pier, which at that time was the logo for the Chicago Convention & Visitors Bureau. It was sitting on a table at the end of the row, and there was this gorgeous, tall, Black woman smiling and shaking people's hands. I did not know her name, but I knew I wanted to be friends with her immediately. I walked up to Lisa, introduced myself, and said, "I moved to Chicago about fifteen years ago and can't believe I have not met you yet, but I'll be back in Chicago in a year, and I just have a feeling that you and I are going to be friends." From that moment on, we have been pals. When I found out that Lisa's dad had been a Harlem Globetrotter, I was over the moon. My dad took us to many sporting events over the years, but one of my favorite things to do was to go see the Harlem Globetrotters at Madison Square Garden!

If you have ever played in a golf scramble, you know that typically you must use everyone's drive twice. Driving is the best part of my game, though my dad and my Uncle Whitey always said, "Drive for show, putt for dough!"

On the day of the MPI New Jersey golf outing, neither Dawn nor I

And Then...

had great drives on the first two holes. Typically, I am a back nine gal. My partner said to Dawn's husband, "Maybe we should get the ladies' shots out of the way now?" within earshot of me and Dawn. We were ready to kill him. Snide remarks like this ensued for the rest of the day until I could not take it anymore. I finally said, "I find you very offensive." As soon as the words were out of my mouth, I sort of regretted them. It was true, but he was my guest. Still, his arrogance and disregard for women golfers was driving us nuts. When he had a great drive a few holes later, I fell all over myself telling him what a great shot he had. "Way to go!" He replied in a staccato voice: "Margie, isn't that the objective of the game, to hit the fairways and the greens?" I cringed and tried to avoid speaking to him for the rest of the day to keep my blood pressure in check. Kind of hard when you are sharing a golf cart though!

At the turn, I went to use the ladies' room, which was *packed*. I did not know a soul. Sitting on the toilet, feeling very upset, I could not contain myself and yelled out, "Has anyone ever played with a guy who treats women golfers so badly you want to scream?" A woman in line yelled back, "Sounds like you're playing with Joe Blow to me!" I said, "How do you know?" She said, "Because I played with that asshole last year!" I learned that usually, a leopard does not change its spots!

That same day, however, after the golf ended, they had happy hour and a dinner. I showered and changed and put on a casual sundress. I found myself a glass of white wine and was chatting with some folks when I heard a familiar voice. It reminded me of someone I had not seen since I was a child. I followed the sound and saw a grown woman with several men around her chatting and laughing. I walked over to where she was and checked her nametag to make sure I was right. Cathy Reynolds had been on the Red Team with me at camp. I remembered that she was a great athlete and super nice and fun. I walked up to her and said, "I think you are the same Cathy who was on the Red Team with me at Our Lady of Lourdes Camp. I'm right, aren't I?" She looked me right in the eye and said, "Yes, Margie McCartney, it's me," and we hugged and reminisced and laughed. We had not seen each other in thirty years, but it did not matter.

Once, when working for the Educational Foundation of the NRA in the 1990s, I was attending a meeting at the Swan and Dolphin in Orlando. President George H. W. Bush was there, and we all had our photos taken with him the first evening after the opening dinner.

The next day was a golf outing at the resort, and my foursome ended up being directly behind the president's foursome. I was playing with three men I did not know, who after our initial drives said, "We can't go; we'll hit into them." I said, "I can go. I'll never hit it that far." I proceeded to crush the ball, sending it well over 200 yards right down the fairway into the president's foursome. The Secret Service agent picked up my ball, slowly turned around, appeared to make a sour face, and threw my ball back at me.

I yelled back, "Best shot of my life!" flashing a proud smile. What a great, lifelong golf story!

And Then...

While working for the NRA Ed Foundation, I was also fortunate enough to attend the Tennessee Restaurant Association golf outing in Nashville several times. This particular year, maybe 1998, I invited a guy from our office, who had done a lot of extra projects for me, to play in our foursome at the TRA golf outing at the Hermitage Golf Course in Old Hickory, TN. We were playing in a foursome with my buddy Adam Ashcraft, who was a trainer for the TRA and hilarious. We'd become friends in the first few seconds that we met several years earlier. Adam is a tall, powerful guy with a great smile and easy golf swing.

They inserted a fourth person that we did not know into our group when someone else had to drop out. All I remember was that his name was Dick. Appropriate name, though we did not know that initially. It was best ball as usual, and after the first hole or two, Dick says to the three of us, "Since I am the best golfer, why don't I go first? Then you guys can try to do better than me."

WHAAAAAAAAAAAAAAT? We just looked at each other and burst out laughing. On every tee moving forward, we just cheered, "Show us what you got, *Dick*!" or "You the Man, Dick!" He tried to cozy up to us at the lunch, but we were having none of that.

The best part of this is that Dick sold industrial refrigerator cleaning and Adam owned a restaurant, at the time, called the Painted Table in Knoxville. A few weeks later, Adam returned from an errand to the restaurant and his staff told him that his friend Dick

Golf

from the TRA golf outing came by to see if he was interested in buying the industrial refrigerator cleaning for their restaurant refrigerators. Adam took the brochure Dick left behind, ripped it in half in front of everyone in the room, and told his staff, "We will *never* do business with *Dick*!" After all, what goes around does, in fact, come around.

When I was the Association Sales Manager at the NRA Educational Foundation in the 1990s, Michael Johnson became our boss and we felt so lucky. He treated us so well and was always incredibly supportive. We all loved him, and we all loved to golf. I was the only female Sales Manager. We all had our own sales teams and traveled *a lot*! Our sales numbers were consistently impressive, and we all got along well. It was a great time while it lasted, for sure.

Michael and I played golf at many events over the years, and he always told me that I drove a golf cart like Erwin Rommel, the Desert Fox. He is probably right. One time, he was driving, I think we were in Tennessee, and for some reason I was wearing all white that day. It had been raining and the grass was wet. I think we just took "Cart Path Only" to be a suggestion.

I was exiting the cart on the right side, and the tip of my golf shoe got caught in the small lip on the side of the floor, and I fell out of the cart on all fours, getting mud all over me and my white outfit. We laughed so hard; I may have wet my pants. Then a lightning warning blared, and we had to go inside, which was probably best at that point.

On several occasions, Michael Johnson would invite the four of us to his and his awesome wife Ann Weiser's great house in Galena for a "meeting." Their house is located on the grounds of Galena Territory with many great golf courses close by. We got to play the General and several other spectacular courses over the years after our meetings to review goals and strategies. Galena is always a special destination.

At one point, I was speaking to my counterparts on the sales team, John, Mike, and Jim, and we realized two of us were going to be in New York City at the same time for work. I suggested that the others join us that Friday and we make a weekend out of it golfing, and that we could all stay at my parents' house.

That evening, we went to a local spot in Pelham for dinner and returned to my folks' back patio for a nightcap. I had the "great idea" that we should practice our tee shots right there and then. We grabbed our golf clubs and lined up on my parents' front lawn facing the Pelham Country Club and teed up some golf balls around midnight. I wish I had a video of the four of us, because it must have looked hilarious. Mind you, I was in a pink-flowered flowy dress, and my neighbors woke up to the sound of our roaring laughter. They saw us the next morning and were about to say something in front of my dad when I interrupted them and scurried us off for our next adventure, so as not to get in trouble. The tennis courts were in front of my parents' house as well as the eighteenth tee box, but the seventeenth hole fairway was a bit to the right. Pretty sure most of our golf balls ended up on the tennis courts, and I remember thinking that whoever showed

Golf

up to play tennis the next day at the Pelham Country Club must have thought there were a *lot* of novice golfers playing the day before!

That next day, my gracious Godfather, Ned Weihman, who belonged to Round Hill in Greenwich, was kind enough to invite us to be his guests for lunch and eighteen holes. It was spectacular! My friends were very impressed, and I was very appreciative. Afterward, we showered and changed and headed into NYC. It was an action-packed weekend for sure and one I reflect upon with a big smile!

My friend Margaret O'Donnell used to caddy for tournaments all around Chicago with her sister Ann when they were young. One weekend, we were up in Lake Geneva and the two of us decided to play a round of golf at Geneva National. I hit my ball in the FUKAWI grass (vernacular for *Where the "F" Are We?*) and saw an apple on the ground nearby. I said to Margaret, "I wonder what would happen if I hit this apple with my driver." Margaret said, "Oh, Margie, you don't want to do that. I have seen someone do it before and the apple will go all over you." Thinking she did not know what she was talking about, I started to practice swing through the apple, saying, "No, Margaret, if I hit the apple and follow through correctly, the apple will go flying forward." She smiled, condescendingly (which I deserved). I swung through the apple. Yup, she was right. I had apple in my eyes, nose, and ears and all over my face. Beet red, I cleaned myself off and never challenged Margaret on anything golf related again.

And Then...

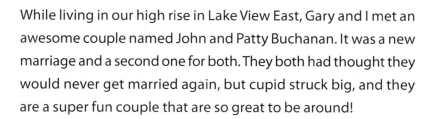

While living in our high rise in Lake View East, Gary and I met an awesome couple named John and Patty Buchanan. It was a new marriage and a second one for both. They both had thought they would never get married again, but cupid struck big, and they are a super fun couple that are so great to be around!

Last year they started their move to Texas but spent several months first at John's house in Galena, Illinois. Gary and I went out to visit last summer for a weekend and had a blast. We loved their home and played golf and hit up a winery over the weekend. Friday evening, while Patty grilled us burgers on the first night, I was looking at the wall of fame in their kitchen and saw a black and white photo of his grandfather. I asked about him, and John rolled his eyes and made one of those faces that you know means, "This is going to be a long story." I refilled my beverage and joined them on the patio for what was, in fact, an incredible story.

His grandfather was a businessman. He wanted to divorce his very Catholic wife who was beside herself when, after he moved out, he served her with divorce papers. She was supposed to show up at the courthouse in the Chicago suburbs on a certain date to sign the divorce papers, but she called her husband so distraught that he went over and ripped up the papers and told her not to worry about it. She just thought that was the end of it. She had no idea that he had, in fact, divorced her and remarried another woman!

Golf

Sometime later, John's grandfather, B. Buchanan, and three of his male friends went to golf at Tam O' Shanter Golf Course on the north side. After playing eighteen holes, they sat down for lunch and had some cocktails. Two of the men were going to play another round of golf with their wives in the afternoon. The other man, with John's grandfather, had recently purchased a WWII trainer plane and thought it would be cool if he and John's grandfather went flying over the golf course and dipped their wing to their friends golfing with their wives. Feeling no pain, they took off and did just that. But then, they ended up crashing in the woods nearby and were both killed.

Mrs. Buchanan number one only found out about Mrs. Buchanan number two when they both showed up to the morgue to claim the body!

Rick Hud is a hospitality professional whom I had the good fortune to meet when I first moved to Chicago and worked at the Knickerbocker Hotel in the early 1990s. He was great pals with my first boss, Jean, from the" Knick" as we affectionately called it. When I first met him, he worked for Prince Resorts in Hawaii. When MPI was in Hawaii in the early 1990s, I got a complimentary stay at his hotel for the length of the conference, and in return Jean would give their sales folks comp rooms at the Knickerbocker when in town on business.

Rick and I have both had the honor of winning the MPI (Meeting Professionals International) Supplier of the Year Award in Chica-

And Then...

go. Rick is a class act and someone you just automatically want to hug because he is sweet and gracious. For the past several years, while I was with PRA and he was with the San Francisco Travel Association, he was kind enough to invite me to be his guest to play in the Friends of Marlene (FOM) Golf Outing, held in autumn. I did not know Marlene Hetzel Palmerson, but she sure seems like someone I wish I had known! My friend, Mary Patton, is involved with this organization as well and said Marlene was a wonderful human being. She was in the hospitality industry for a long time before she lost her battle with cancer, and was known for her kindhearted, compassionate nature and for always putting client relationships first. Those are qualities that we all try to emulate. This golf outing was a big fundraiser that supported Gilda's Club Chicago, an organization that raises funds for programs to support anyone impacted by cancer. The foursomes were expensive, it was an awesome event, and I was honored to be included.

My first year playing at the FOM outing, Rick also invited Tim Mulkeen, a Director of Meetings for a financial services company, to play in our foursome. Their conference later that year was in San Fran, so he and Rick and I were all involved with that great program. Tim is also a terrific golfer, a proud Pittsburgh man, and a super guy. The three of us have played together several other times as well. I always learn something new golfing with them!

At the Chicago MPI golf outing in 2008, I was about to sit down with my guest, Jay Hirt, for breakfast. A handsome man sat alone at a table, and I asked if we could join him. His name was Paul Campbell. He had a great smile and a Southern accent, and I asked where he was from. He said originally Tennessee, but that he had recently moved from South Carolina to Chicago as he married a girl from Chicago in the hospitality industry. I asked who and he said, "Inge Spindola." I immediately replied, "Though I don't know Inge that well, I do know that she has a great reputation and everyone who knows her loves her, so you must be a great guy too!"

Soon after, we were together with Inge at an industry event and she mentioned that she was traveling out of town the next weekend and if there was anything fun going on in town, if I would include Paul. On the spot, I invited him to a pre-Cubs game BBQ at my home, and although I did not have an extra ticket for the game, I told him that we would have a group getting together in Wrigleyville after the game if he wanted to join us. And so, our friendship was born and to this day they are two of my favorite people!

And Then… I remembered how important it is to extend yourself to someone alone.

Have you ever been alone wishing someone would come up and introduce themselves to you?

Have you ever gone out of *your* way to make someone else feel comfortable?

I promise you, giving first makes you feel great and you usually end up making a new friend.

And Then...

Golfing with Margaret O'Donnell.

Singing the National Anthem with Patty Tait at Camden Yards (June 2001).

Stuck at a train station in Europe hoping to make it safely to my next destination (1981).

Chapter Thirteen

Go With Your Gut

In 1995, my friend Jim O'Donnell introduced me to Sharon Pannozzo, who was the Director of Media Relations for the Chicago Cubs. Having sung in several choirs over the years and having been a regular at karaoke bars in NYC in my younger days, I thought it would be cool to try to sing the national anthem at Wrigley Field. I solicited interest from an old college friend named Jae (JT), to see if she might want to try to do a duet with me. I figured we could go to the Old Town School of Folk Music and find someone who could write us a cool harmony. We did just that. She sang the melody, and I had a harmony that sort of chased her, and it sounded great. Super psyched, I sent the tape to Sharon, and she got us set up to sing on my thirty-fifth birthday, June 8, 1996. It was a night game, and the fog was brutal, you could barely see behind second base! Also, it was unseasonably cold that night; felt more like late October. About 300 friends and family flew in from around the country to cheer us on. Then there was a birthday party across the street upstairs at a bar that was big fun afterward.

Because of Sharon's kindness, we got to sing at Wrigley another time, a year or two later. It was on a Sunday, so we also sang "God Bless America," which was a thrill as well. After Wrigley,

Go With Your Gut

I started sending our audition tape to other MLB teams. We ended up singing at games for the Chicago White Sox, San Francisco Giants, Baltimore Orioles, Pittsburgh Pirates, New York Mets, and Boston Red Sox.

I worked hard and ended up getting many dates lined up for us, and my efforts paid off as we have memories for a lifetime. I know that National Anthem run will be in my obituary one day. On my fortieth birthday weekend, we were scheduled to sing at Camden Yards in Baltimore. JT threw her back out and could not fly from Chicago. My buddy Allen Tait and his awesome wife Patty by this point had moved from Chicago to the Baltimore suburbs.

I knew Patty had sung at several weddings before, so I called and asked her if she would stand in and sing the melody at the ballpark that weekend. She kindly agreed and I FedEx-ed her a tape so she could practice. When I arrived in Baltimore and got to their home, we practiced over and over that day in the backyard. She nailed it! Also, before the game, we went to a bar across the street from Camden Yards to give it a practice shot with the locals. Good thing we did, because it scared us when in the second round of, "Oh Say, does that Star Spangled banner yet wave…" the fans all yelled "OH" really loud and made the sign of an O with their fingers (for Orioles). It completely caught us off guard. However, when we were on the field later that evening, when it came to that part of the song, we made the symbol and emphasized the O to be a part of the hometown crowd! One decision to go for it, to trust your gut that you can do something, can change the resume of your life.

And Then...

There are some stories that you never tell your parents, even years later. I figure if no one got hurt, in the end, it is okay. When I was nineteen and doing my semester abroad in Bregenz, Austria, there were two things that happened that I did not tell my parents about for probably twenty-five years. One incident happened in Killiney, Ireland, the other in Luxembourg.

After Christmas, I took a train to Le Havre, France, to catch a boat to Rosslare Harbor in Ireland to meet up with my friend Tom Hopkins, a.k.a. Hopper, and his Fairfield University friends, Slick and Spo. Slick had an uncle who owned a weaver shop in Killiney, which is why we decided to meet up there. Hop, Slick, Spo, and I are all from Irish descent, and it was exciting to be going there for the first time. They had arrived before me, so I made my way to meet them.

I had been told that you could catch a free ride from the lorry drivers at the Le Havre docks as they board the ferry. So, that is what I did for passage from Le Havre, France, as money was tight. Once on the boat, I figured I could just find a place to crash in a chair or something, as we would be in Ireland in the morning. However, it was very cold, and I get seasick. Any travel motion, really, makes me sick, but the waters of the English Channel were particularly rough that night.

I was sitting in the front of the boat and chatting with strangers and soon realized with each new swell that I was going to be sick. Some of the lorry drivers took pity on me and got me into a bunk in their room and held back my hair while I got sick in the sink. I was embarrassed but was so excited for my first trip to Ireland that I tried to stay positive even though I sort of wanted to die at the same time.

The next morning, I woke up and several of the many lorry drivers in rows of bunk beds were staring at me saying, "American Girl, American Girl, wake up! Is it true like they show on Dynasty and Dallas on TV that all American men have three mistresses?" This is what they wanted to know?! I laughed and said that although I was sure some did, it was not something I was familiar with in my life. My parents were crazy about each other, and fidelity was never an issue at home. However, no marriage is perfect and my mom shared years later that from time to time, she did consider murder, but never divorce.

The first thing I did when I got to Ireland was to look through the phone book at the docks at Rosslare Harbor to see how many McCartneys there were. Ireland is about the size of Ohio, and I was disappointed when I saw that there were maybe three listings in all of Ireland with our spelling. Tons of McCarthys though. Years later when my sister and I went to Scotland on vacation, we checked out museums in Edinburgh and looked up our name. In the War Museum, we found tons of McCartneys and many Archibald McCartneys for some reason. My dad had always told us that our name changed from Macartney to McCartney at Ellis Island. It could have been a clerical error.

And Then...

I made my way to Killiney to connect with Hopper and Slick. We found a pub and watched a John Wayne movie called *The Green Beret's* that first afternoon. The movie theme song was stuck in my mind for months.

After the movie, we ordered an early dinner. Oxtail soup did not sound so great, but it was delicious with a slice of bread and butter! While there, someone told us about a youth hostel a few miles away that would be a good place for us to stay for the night. Since it had pretty much been raining the entire time I had been in Ireland, I put my backpack near the fireplace to dry. While I was petting the owner's dog, I smelled something burning and realized it was my backpack that was too close to the fireplace! The damage was minimal, and we laughed about it. Then, Hopper (who later worked for the Secret Service and then the FBI) and his buddy Slick (who several years later became a priest) thought if we split up hitchhiking, we would get to the youth hostel faster. Though I had never hitchhiked before and was a bit leery, since my traveling companions thought it was a good idea, I figured (with nothing but beer and oxtail soup in my tummy) that yeah, sure…sounds okay. Maybe that is why the suggestion that I go first because someone would be more likely to pick up a girl and then I could say, "Can we stop for my friends?" did not seem too outlandish at that moment.

I headed out on the road in the dark and the rain with my slightly burned backpack and Irish cap on. A man pulled up and asked me where I was headed, and I told him to the youth hostel a few miles down the road. He said he could drop me off. I was thrilled to get out of the rain and pulled the passenger seat back so I could put my backpack in the back seat. Then he said he needed to make a stop first… hmmmm…and drove into the woods.

My heart sank and my mind was like a pinball machine. Of course, that familiar refrain went through my brain: "If I die, my parents will kill me!" That, and "NEVER GET IN A CAR WITH STRANGERS," which of course we had all known to be a mantra since childhood. He asked me if I liked to drink before having sex, and if I wanted some scotch. He had a bottle. I told him that the two guys I was hitchhiking with were linebackers from Notre Dame University and if I did not get to the youth hostel in the next few minutes, they would be calling the police. I figured if he grabbed me, I would open the door and literally run for my life. I just kept mentioning the police and he eventually drove back up the road. When I saw streetlights again, I figured I would live to see another sunrise.

He dropped me at the youth hostel and said, "I'll be driving back into town in an hour if you want me to pick you up?" I ran to the front door of the youth hostel in tears. Hopper and Slick were already checking in at the front desk and when I blurted out what had happened, the woman at registration immediately called the police. When the police arrived and I told them what had just transpired, they said, "Aren't you an American? Don't you know not to get into a car with strangers?

I naively replied, "I would never do this at home, but I thought everyone in Ireland was nice." I remembered the car was

And Then...

brown and two door and that he was about forty (seemed so old at the time). He had brown eyes that I saw when an oncoming car's lights shined into his car. They seemed to know who he was, a local, because this was something he did often. However, he had never actually hurt anyone that they knew of, and he did not force me into the car. I went willingly, happy and eager to get out of the rain. I decided never to hitchhike again!

So, the next story from this same semester abroad may come as a surprise after reading the first one, but...I went with my gut. My journey home to the USA was crazy! First, I took a train close to Nordlingen, Germany, to spend the night at the Kortenhoffs, who used to work for my grandfather. Then the next night, I had to take a train to Stuttgart where I switched to go to Saarbrucken, where I switched to get to Trier, where I slept on a bench in the train station. When I got to the Luxembourg Airport for my return flight to Kennedy Airport on Icelandair, it was Sunday, Jan 24, 1982. I had called Icelandair in Vienna to confirm that I was booked on a flight that night. But unfortunately, that lady lied to me. At the airport, I found out that there were no flights out until Tuesday, January 26. I had no money, no cell phone, no credit cards. I was nineteen years old. A woman at the counter could see how upset I was and said that although the youth hostel was closed, there was a religious house for young women to stay and it was supposed to be cheap. I shoved what I could of my luggage into lockers and just took

Go With Your Gut

a duffle bag with a change of clothes and toiletries and my camera, and off I went.

I took a bus from the airport to the address the lady gave me and rang the bell, but there was no answer. I was ringing the bell of a hotel near the train station (also no answer) when I turned and saw a guy that looked like he might speak English. He did! Eager to find someone who might be able to help me, I said hello and explained what had happened to me. He could see how upset I was and offered to buy me a coffee at a nearby café. His name was Chris, and he was a biochemist from England. He walked around the area to see if there was anything that looked decent that I could afford. (I told him I was at the end of my trip and end of my money). After five months of meeting strangers, I felt like I had become a pretty good judge of character and he seemed nice, so I said, "If I hadn't left my sleeping bag at the airport, I would ask you if I could crash on your floor!" He replied that he had a bed and if I trusted him, I was welcome to stay. He said it was nothing fancy, but I would be safe and warm.

I went with my gut, as he appeared to be calm and kind, and I accepted. That sounded much better than another night on a train station bench. He had a client dinner that night but got me settled at his place first. I took a shower and crashed early. Curled up in a ball, I had my red hoodie bathrobe pulled tight around me so just my nose and mouth were exposed like a red telescope. I was warm, clean, and grateful.

The next day, I went to visit the American Military Cemetery where 5,076 American Soldiers are buried, including General Patton. It gave me chills to read all the monuments of gratitude to those Americans who gave their lives for world peace. I saw Dad's infantry (the 87th) marked on the monument by St. Vith, which is where he was shot in Belgium. That second night, Chris took me out to dinner and then introduced me to some of his British friends who had also recently relocated to Luxembourg. He made sure I got on the right bus to the airport the next morning and as he hugged me goodbye, he told me that he was going to write a book about me. I smiled, grateful to be alive, never in a million years thinking *I* would be writing a book one day and sharing this story. I knew I had a guardian angel on my shoulder.

Dad died in June 2005. That fall, I asked my Chicago friend Jen Kramer if she wanted to come to New York and go to a Giants game with me. To this day, Jen and I are never completely sure how we met, but we knew when we saw each other at Mass at Old St. Patrick's Church one day in downtown Chicago that we knew each other. We think it was from attending a Landmark seminar together in the early 1990s. Jen is a spectacular human being. She ran for Alderman of the forty-third ward in 2016, and I proudly rang doorbells for her. In 2018 she decided to make it the "Year of Love" and every day she would post a story on Facebook about a stranger she met, someone she saw doing something kind, or highlighting a friendship that was special to her. Eventually, she was featured in the Chicago Tribune and interviewed on television because her stories made such an impact.

Jen is also a champion of the Special Olympics. I think she has raised almost $50,000 for the Chicago Chapter of Special Olympics, and her costumes for the Polar Plunge every year are notorious.

The tagline under her photo on Facebook reads "Love Fiercely, because this all ends." It would be next to impossible not to adore Jen Kramer! I told her that she could bring a friend along to the Big Apple and we could stay at my sister's apartment at 72nd Street and Broadway. Mary went to Mom's for the weekend so we could use her place.

We were crossing Amsterdam Avenue to catch a cab heading north to a Piano Bar I had heard about. It was Christmas time in the Big Apple, and it was cold, and you could hear the bell ringer on the corner for the Salvation Army by the outdoor florist that was now selling Christmas trees. It smelled like pine and started to snow. For a moment, it felt like a Hallmark holiday movie!

It was odd that I looked down and saw a small white dog crossing the street with no leash or person. I thought it was strange, but at the same time I saw a taxi and started to run in hopes of grabbing it, anxious to get our evening started. A man got there first and hopped into the cab. I was bummed he beat me to it. I stood on the corner waiting for this cab to pull out and the next one to pull up. Then I noticed a European-looking and sounding man with an olive-colored corduroy jacket pick up the white dog and stand in front

And Then...

of the cab beside me where the passenger had just gotten in the back seat. The man with the dog pointed at the man in the back seat and yelled, "That man robbed me. He took my watch!" The cab driver turned and looked at the man in the back seat and thought that I should help the man in the jacket, who was frantic. I opened up the back seat of the cab and said to the man, "What do you think you are doing? Give me the watch!" This man's eyes grew wide as saucers and I am sure he was thinking, *Who is this crazy lady?* But he gave me the watch, which I threw on the hood of the car for the man with the dog. He took the watch and shouted, "And he took my wallet!"

I said to the man in the back seat, "Give me the wallet," and he did. I threw that on the hood of the car and olive-corduroy jacket man picked it up. At this point it almost felt like a game show, until...the man with the dog said, "And he knifed me!" That was when I backed up to Andy's Deli on Amsterdam and 72nd street and motioned to the robber he was clear to leave. I was done being the hero. He ran south through oncoming traffic headed north, and the man in the olive jacket with the dog chased him screaming, "Call the police!"

I dialed 411 by mistake, but once I heard "City and State" I was like...ugh, wrong number. So, I dialed 911 for the first time in my life and gave them a quick recap of what had happened. Suddenly, I saw a cop car go after the thief and thought....my work here is done. Jennifer, her friend, and I took a cab to the East Side for our date with a piano bar.

Go With Your Gut

The tailgating on Sunday at Meadowlands was fun and the Giants beat the Cowboys, which is always a season highlight! Then on Monday, Mom had organized an early Christmas luncheon with her friends in Pelham and my sister came too. I shared this story at lunch because I felt good about helping a stranger. My mom loved the story. My sister hated this story and that day said to me, "Mommy just buried Daddy. What if we had to bury you too?" I said I was sorry it upset her but knew if I had to do it again, I would. My thinking was that the man who had been robbed and knifed could have been someone in my family or a friend of mine, and I would hope that someone would help them.

Fast forward to three months later. I got a phone call from the District Attorney's office of the City of New York. The woman asked me if I had witnessed a crime on Friday night, December 2 in NYC. I said, "Well I am a Law and Order Groupie...it took you long enough to find me!" to which she replied that her boss had told her to check the 911 tapes and that is how she tracked me down. They wanted me to testify, and although I was nervous, I said I would. It never came to that, though, because they caught the guy and when they told him that I could identify him along with his victim, he admitted his guilt. I asked if the man with the dog and olive corduroy blazer had really been stabbed because I had not seen any blood on his white, shirt, and she said yes and that he was very appreciative of what I had done but was too busy chasing the robber down Amsterdam to stop and thank me.

I ended up getting a letter of thanks from the City of New

York saying that the thief was behind bars for seven years and then would be on probation for another five, because of my actions. It may have been risky, but I was glad that I took a chance and helped a stranger.

And Then... It feels good to go out on a limb for someone. I have always felt that we must take care of each other in this world.

Have you ever had a situation where you went out of your way to help a stranger and it felt great?

I have been on both sides of that giving and receiving. Both feel great.

Have you ever trusted someone, and it backfired? Although that experience may cause you to think twice about trusting, don't quit trying to help people.

Remember life offers two great things: time and the ability to choose how we spend it.

One Thing Leads to Another

Gary and I met Doug Guller, from Austin, Texas at an outdoor restaurant on 4th Street in Cleveland before game six of the 2016 World Series. We all stayed for game seven after the Cubs victory and we have been friends ever since!

Chapter Fourteen

One Thing Leads to Another

The first friend I made after moving to Chicago on December 4, 1989, was Margaret O'Donnell, who at the time was the Director of the Reservations Department at the Knickerbocker Chicago Hotel on Walton Street. We became friends over the phone before I even moved to Chicago, as I had a lead for her for a meeting and was checking availability. As soon as she answered the phone, "Reservations, this is Margaret O'Donnell, how many I help you?" I was like, "Margaret O'Donnell, my name is Margie McCartney, and I am from NY. I just accepted a job as the Corporate Sales Manager at your hotel and I bet we are going to be fast friends."

As Margaret and I quickly became friends, she shared that her sister Ann had died a few years earlier due to an undiagnosed heart defect. Though I had never met Ann O'Donnell, this story made me know that I would have *loved* her too. Margaret shared that when Ann was in high school, she had told her parents she was staying at a friend's house overnight. That same friend told her parents that she was staying at the O'Donnells' house that same Saturday night in Old Norwood Park. There was some big party in another suburb far away that they wanted to go to. Sunday morning, Mrs. O'Donnell called the girlfriend's house to

One Thing Leads to Another

see if Ann wanted to go to Mass with them. She was calling to offer to pick her up, but the friend's mom said, "Ann, isn't here. Our daughter said she slept at your house last night?" BUSTED. When Ann got home, her dad said, "Young lady, where were you last night?" Ann confessed that they had wanted to go to a fun party in the suburbs and were afraid her parents wouldn't let her go, so she and her friend had made up a plan. He said, "Get in the car and take me to where the party was!" She had no idea what town or what address the party was at, but knew she could not say Old Norwood Park, where they lived, because her dad knew everyone in town. They got on a highway and drove for twenty minutes or so when she said, "I think it was around here," so Mr. O'Donnell exited. They drove around the same neighborhood about four times when Ann noticed a girl around her age talking on the front porch with whom she assumed were her parents. Her dad was like, "I know you are making this all up. Where were you last night?" Ann said, "I think it's that house over there," where she had seen the girl her age. Her father said, "You go in there and get your friend and bring her out here!"

Ann went up to the porch of the house, but the girl had already gone back inside. She asked the parents if she could speak with their daughter and they said, "She is just in the kitchen." So, Ann goes inside the house and says to the stranger in the kitchen, "Listen, I know you do not know me, but I lied to my parents last night and told them I was at a party in this town. When I saw you, you looked nice, so I am hoping I might be able to use you as a scapegoat as I'm in big trouble." The girl laughed and said, "Sure, what do you need me to do?" Ann said I know this sounds crazy, but will you come outside to see my dad in the car? He will probably give you a brief lecture, but then we'll be gone."

I swear to this day, I wish I knew this girl's name and number because I would totally call her up and invite her to do something fun as a thank you!

So, the girl goes out to Mr. O'Donnell's car and he says, "Young lady, I can't believe that you hosted an underage party here last night and you are lucky I don't go up and tell your parents what you did!" The stranger apologized to Mr. O'Donnell and said, "It won't happen again, sir." Ann hugged her and got in the car and waved goodbye, never to see each other again.

Both women are my kind of gals! People can be so awesome!

When my nephew Charlie was about eight years old, I scored some great seats right behind home plate for an afternoon Cubs game against the New York Mets. I root for the Mets when they are not playing the Chicago Cubs. By chance, we sat next to a man named Frank Cheswick wearing full Mets gear. Naturally, as a native New Yorker, I introduced myself and my nephew. Charlie was born a die-hard Cubs fan, and every time Frank would cheer for the Mets, Charlie would punch him in the arm. Not too hard and it was kind of funny. I was working for the NRA Ed Foundation at the time, and Frank worked at Bankers Trust across the street from my office on Wacker Drive in the Sears Tower. We really connected as New Yorkers tend to do, and he was kind enough to invite me to his office for lunch a few weeks later. I remember leaving that lunch hoping that I would know this great guy for a long time. One of the most attractive things about any man is when they adore their wives. If I meet a man who is married and always checking out and flirting with other women, it always upsets me. It's not attractive; it's ugly. But show me a guy who brags about how great his wife and kids are and there is someone I usually treasure as a friend. Frank is that kind of a man.

Several years later when I worked for a start-up that stopped, I was looking for a new job. I called Frank to see if he knew anyone in the hospitality industry I might want to speak with. Frank introduced me to his friend Rick Connor, who was the Director of Sales for a hotel rep company called DGO. I walked into my interview and immediately thought Rick looked like Pierce Brosnan with a strong Boston accent. We connected right away, chatted like we were old friends and then he said "Mahgie McCahteny, you're hired!

"He and his lovely wife, Renee, are parents to Courtney, who is off to college next year. Rick, like Frank, is someone who adores his wife and is beyond proud of his daughter. Hard to believe I worked for him when she was born. I remember he had to go away on a business trip, and Courtney was just an infant and Renee did not want to be home alone, so they asked me if I would spend the night at their place, so she would not be by herself. I was honored. Several years later, Rick started his own business, Meeting Your Needs, and moved to Scottsdale, AZ, where he works from a home office and Renee works for Chase. Their house is gorgeous and is right on Grey Hawk golf course. I have stayed with them many times. After my dad died, my mom and

And Then...

sister and I were in Arizona, and they invited us over for dinner. It was my dad's birthday (January 14), so we sent balloons to heaven from their backyard, poolside, which meant a lot to me.

We were on that trip in Arizona due to the kindness of Lisa Pettorossi, who worked in the Sales Department for the Westin Kierland Resort and Spa in Scottsdale, which we had represented at DGO. She was thoughtful enough to offer me a house on the golf course, free, for a long weekend for my mom and sister and me to stay at. I had booked some nice programs at the property over the years and that was her way of saying thank you. She is no longer there, but we keep in touch, and she is a terrific person.

I spent two years at DGO and will always be grateful to Rick Connor for that opportunity, as I learned a lot from him. Most importantly, when I would walk into his office upset about a situation, he would say to me, "Play out the Tape." Meaning, for every action, there is a reaction. So, If I say or do "xyz," the other person will probably do or say what? It was a great lesson and I try to incorporate it still to this day in my life. (Have not mastered it yet though!) Initially, we had small offices downtown in the American Library Association Building at 40 East Huron St., which we were leasing. Then we moved to new offices on Orleans St. off Chicago Avenue, and they were big, new, and beautiful. One of the best things about the location was that it was kitty corner from Club Lago, which is an awesome Italian Restaurant that I had never heard of before but quickly fell in love with! I took my folks there too and they felt the same way. Club Lago opened in 1952. Initially, their vision was to provide Northern Italian food to the printers and paper salesmen who worked in the warehouse district around Superior and Orleans. It has red and white checked tablecloths, a bar you would expect The Rat Pack to hang out at, and the owners and brothers, Guido and Giancarlo Nardini, are always welcoming and generous!

And then... I realized that if I had not gone to the Cubs game that day, I would have probably never met Frank, which means I would not have met Rick. I would not have gotten that job and might never have made so many amazing hotel connections around the globe that led me to my next opportunity, which led me to my next opportunity...and so it goes.

When we were young on Bon Mar Road, our neighbors, the Regans, had a German Shephard named Rex. Though he was chained in their yard when outside, the chain was long. My sister, Mary, was cutting through another neighbor's backyard on the way home from school one day and Rex bit her in the butt and she had to get stiches. Remember this!

Will Regan was born on the same day I was, and we had our first co-ed birthday party together when we turned thirteen. I was Class Clown our senior year at PMHS and he was Most Likely to Succeed. Will had done great in the hospitality industry in NYC, and over the years owned and managed many popular, high-end nightclubs. Years later, my mom cut out an article from the newspaper that Will had opened a place on the West side called REX!

Fast Forward about ten years. I had just moved to Chicago when a major airline carrier had a new promotion offering discounted flights on a trial route from Midway. I cannot remember exactly, but I think it was buy one ticket, get one free. I decided to invite my friend Margaret O'Donnell to Pelham to be with my family for Easter.

It was a zoo at the new Midway Airport, and I remember the lady at the counter said, "If everyone would just shut up and sit down, maybe we could get you all out of here." Lovely! Also, they served burgers on Good Friday on the flight home to LaGuardia, which seemed odd, but whatever. The plan upon arriving in NYC was to stay at my sister's apartment in Manhattan and meet up with a bunch of friends at Puglia's in Little Italy for dinner that night.

After dinner, Margaret and I and maybe one or two others were in a cab heading back to the apartment when I happened to glance left out my window and saw REX in huge letters and yelled, "STOP THE CAB!" It was late at this point and the line to get into this club was down the block and heading toward the Hudson River, but I figured since I knew the owner, I could try to VIP us and sauntered to the front of the line to speak to the bouncer.

In an instant, I decided to steal my sister's story and told him that Will Regan and I shared the same birthday and that I knew the bar was named after his dog Rex because he had bit *me* in the butt as a kid in our neighborhood and I had the stitches to prove it. The guy laughed and said that Will was not there that night, but since I clearly knew Will well, he let us right in and bought us a round of drinks! The Bon Mar Road connection never fails!

One Thing Leads to Another

One day in the summer of 2016, my husband and I were at Wrigley Field in our usual spot in the last row of the bleachers in section 504. I could feel someone's eyes on me. I turned around and saw a strawberry blonde woman/ photographer zooming in on what I later found out were my earrings. She was standing in the VIP private section behind the bleachers in center field with her arm and camera leaning over the railing. As a *huge* Cubs/baseball fan, I was wearing two different earrings. One was a baseball bat, and one was a baseball. I like them, she liked them, and she started shooting photos of them and us.

Her name is Sally Ryan and she was a freelance photographer for the *New York Times* and was assigned the Cubs game that day as we were hopeful to go all the way for the first time in 108 years. I told her that I was originally from New York, and we invited her to join us in the Audi Club after the game. She interviewed us about how we met, etc. and I gave her my business card. She was not sure if the photo would make the paper but said she would reach out when she heard. Several weeks later, she emailed me and said that it was going to be in Sunday's Sports Section on Oct. 9, 2016. Low and behold, there was a great larger shot of a woman's hand with a baseball-themed manicure and bracelet over a scorecard and then next to it, a smaller photo of me (with my earrings) and Gary. Underneath, it mentioned that we had met at a Wrigleyville bar eight years earlier.

I called Mom and Mary in NY. I think they bought out all the local shops of that day's *New York Times*! A copy is framed in our

And Then...

living room.

Several weeks after that, I got a phone call from a woman named Jasmin Shah, another photographer from Chicago. She said she had called her friend Sally Ryan from the *New York Times* to see if she knew of any die-hard Cubs fan couples to be in a photo shoot for her riding a tandem bicycle around Wrigley Field. Sally had given her my info, and a few days later Gary and I met Jasmin at the Wrigleyville Fire Station, where we had dropped off some additional props if needed. She shared that she had done many photo shoots using a family tandem bicycle. One was a restaurant opening where the person in the back was holding a tray with coffee on it, etc. So clever. The tandem bicycle shots were sort of her shtick. Jasmin has since sold everything in Chicago and is traveling the world as a nomad doing documentary projects anywhere she meets people that inspire her. I love following her on Facebook! What a gem!

The photo she took of me and Gary on the tandem bicycle ended up on the cover of Wedding Magazine in Dallas, and a Texas friend sent me a picture of it. We were floored! The original photo is on the cover of this book.

In 2006, for the first Easter since my father had died, I convinced Mom and Mary that we should stay at the Mohonk Mountain House in New Paltz, NY. I had seen this resort advertised at hospitality trade shows for years and always thought it looked *very cool*. We booked it and it was an easy drive from Pelham, may-

177

One Thing Leads to Another

be an hour and a half. The resort consists of about seven different-looking buildings attached to each other. They have lovely grounds and a great spa with floor to ceiling windows looking out over a beautiful forest.

On the first night, we were looking to have a glass of wine at happy hour. The bar was closed for renovations, so we were shown to a suite that was a makeshift bar for the time being at the hotel. We found a group of chairs together and sat down. Pretty quickly, we were laughing loudly, and a big family not too far away heard us and saw we were sitting alone. They said, "You guys seem like fun, please join us!" That is all it took! It was Hugh and Peggy Quigley from Coxsackie, New York south of Albany, and their family. Their daughter Meghan had just gotten married to a guy named Dan Toner on the previous New Year's Eve, so they were newlyweds, and their other son, also Daniel, was married with a baby on the way.

We connected with this great family in such a big way that we planned a vacation together again two years later to Lake George and stayed at the famous Sagamore resort. This was the year, 2008, that Davidson College in North Carolina made it to the elite eight in the NCAA tournament, which was held in Detroit. My oldest brother, John, had gone to Davidson College outside Charlotte and was very active on the Board. You may have heard about a basketball player named Stephen Curry, who played on the Davidson basketball team at the time. Mom was sharing a story with Hugh about how John was a proud Davidson Grad and how he, along with a few other Board members, paid for 800 kids to be bussed from North Carolina, housed in Detroit, and got them all tickets for the game so that Davidson would have

And Then...

a large, enthusiastic presence of support. Hugh Quigley was so impressed by that, at the start our group dinner at the Sagamore that night, he made a toast saluting my brother's generosity and in keeping with that spirit, he said he was picking up dinner for everyone. Generosity is contagious!

My cousin, Meg Walsh, went to Trinity College in Washington, DC. While in DC, she became friends with another New Yorker named Sheila Molloy from Crestwood, New York, who was attending Catholic University.

Years later, Sheila took a pharmaceutical job in Chicago and mentioned to Meg that she was moving to the Windy City! Meg told her that she had to meet her cousin Margie. An Irish gal through and through, I loved Sheila immediately. We catch up several times a year. Last summer, even though COVID-19 was in full swing, we met at a pumpkin patch out on Long Island, had lunch outside at a restaurant, then hit a winery with her family. Fully masked when necessary, of course.

Through Sheila, I met her friend Joe Gallin, also from New York, who lived in Chicago at the same time. Joe is awesome and we all had some fun days in Chicago on the golf course, at Wrigley Field, and many local restaurants and bars. Eventually, Joe moved to LA, where he met his future bride; both worked for ABC sports network. They moved to Connecticut and had two children. Unfortunately, Margaret was diagnosed with cancer. After many treatments, things seemed to be on the mend. They

One Thing Leads to Another

had talked about moving back closer to her family in Chagrin Falls, Ohio, and moved forward with the plan in March 2011. This ended up being fortuitous, as her cancer returned that October. Unfortunately, she lost her battle with that dreaded disease, and Joe is raising his children now and doing an outstanding job. He still works covering golf outings for networks. A handsome fellow with an easy smile, everyone loves being around Joe.

When the Cubs won game five of the World Series on a Sunday night, it was the one home game I did not have tickets to. It was a do or die situation. Prior to the series even starting, I had sold one ticket for game three in the bleachers on Stub Hub for $3500. I was sitting with Kathleen in my other seats in section 222 that night. My husband Gary said, "So, I have to sit alone?" I replied that anyone who would spend that much money on a baseball ticket probably drinks beer and really likes baseball! I suggested he buy them a beer the moment they sat down. It turned out that the guy who bought my ticket had just retired and moved to Florida two weeks earlier. A diehard fan, he told his wife there was no way he was missing going to a game at Wrigley Field if the Cubs were playing in the WORLD SERIES!

Game six was on a Tuesday night in Cleveland. With the money I got selling my bleacher ticket to game three, I bought two round-trip flights on Southwest and two standing-room-only tickets for game six on Stub Hub. We stayed with my friend Joe, and he suggested an area near Progressive Field that would have tons of places to eat pregame. We hoped the train to 4th street and saw an outdoor spot to grab a late lunch/early dinner and went in and sat down to order. The place was packed, and we were dressed from head to toe in Cubs' gear. I tell you, the Cleveland fans were so nice! I was in shock. They kept saying, "Good luck tonight!" As a New Yorker, I could not imagine someone greeting a fan for the other team that way during the World Series! It was refreshing.

A few tables away at a four top, we saw another Cubs fan. He started chatting to us, and we talked about how stoked we were to be there. Soon, he said, "You guys seem fun, why don't you join me?" We said, "Sure" because he was fun too! He was Doug Guller from Austin, Texas. He grew up a Cubs fan and had flown to Chicago for game five. As soon as they won that game, he booked his flight to Cleveland and got the last room at the Marriott downtown, and it was *steep*!

The three of us had standing-room-only tickets. The access to the bar might have been a bit too convenient. We were so jazzed, electricity going through our veins. Once the Cubs went up 7–0 on Addison Russell's grand slam, Doug looked at us and said, "I think the only decision we have now is where are we going to have lunch tomorrow? You both in for tomorrow night's game at $1500 each?" Even though we had a car picking us up at Joe's that next morning at 5 a.m. for a 7 a.m. flight, feeling *no pain*, we said, "YES!" then, seconds later, he looked at Stub Hub on his phone and SRO tickets had just jumped to $1850 each. Were we in? "YES!" Ouch. Though we had just met Doug, he paid for our tickets online and we sent him a check when we got home. Class act.

A friend from Chicago, Stephanie, sent me a Cubs video on Facebook and said, "I think you are in this video?" It was me and Doug

One Thing Leads to Another

jumping up and down with our hands on Gary's shoulders! I showed it to Doug the next day, and Doug was amazed when he noticed that we shared a FB friend—Dan Toner. I had met him with the Quigleys (he is their son-in-law), and Doug was his fraternity brother at Villanova in Philadelphia. Incredible.

From Meg to Sheila to Joe to Doug to Dan and the Quigleys… and the Cubs winning the World Series. Now that is a winning series of connections, for sure.

In 1997, Old St. Patrick's Church in Chicago put together an amazing trip to the Holy Land. I really wanted to go and called my mom and sister Mary in New York to see if they were also interested. They were. I have been on many big planes in my life, but nothing prepared me for the size of the El Al Israel Airlines flight #106. Walking next to the plane, it seemed like we were flying over on the Empire State Building! It was enormous. I still do not understand how something that big can fly.

Our tour was outstanding, and Father Jack Wall was our leader from Old St. Pat's.

We started in Jerusalem and visited Bethlehem, Mount of Olives, Gethsemane, and Bethany. We had an old city walking tour to the Wailing Wall, where so many people were in tears as they shoved their prayers on small pieces of paper into the cracks of the huge stone bricks of the wall. We visited Jericho, the Jordan Valley, Nazareth, Cana, rode a camel, and went on a boat ride on the sea of Galilee. We visited the Mount of Beatitudes. One of the most amazing parts of our journey that stays with me 'til this day was visiting Masada. We took a tramway to get to the top of this mountain, and the ruins there are now a national park.

Soon after all these amazing adventures and with a day or so left on our trip, my sister and I decided to write a song for our bus. We were the Black Bus. There was also the Red and Blue Bus, but we loved our bus, the Black Bus, and it was full of characters. The spiritual leader of our bus was a fine Irishman named Kevin Moran, who was on the journey with his wife Anne. Kevin would recite moving poetry on the bus microphone that would bring us to tears.

And Then… How wonderful that I found Old St. Patrick's Church when I moved to Chicago, that we signed up for this trip, that we shared this amazing adventure…and how one good thing so often leads to another.

Isn't it amazing that so many journeys start with a random meeting?

How could you be more intentional about meeting new people in your day-to-day encounters? One connection usually leads to another, which leads to another.

When Life Gives You Lemons, Sell Them to Buy Wine!

My friend, Jolene Boatright, knows how to always make the best of every situation. Read about Jolene in the next chapter. >>>

Chapter Fifteen

When Life Gives You Lemons, Sell Them to Buy Wine!

(As seen, read, and purchased on cocktail napkins at
Home Spun, a great store in Quogue, New York.)

Winters in Chicago are typically long and cold and snowy. I arrived from New York to the doorstep of the Knickerbocker Hotel on Dec. 4, 1989. It was freezing out. I remember walking down Walton Avenue and the wind was so strong that, as I lifted my leg to take a next step, the wind pushed my leg over a few inches, and I almost fell. My friends back home were saying, "Why are you moving to Chicago in December?" Which made me laugh because New York can get just as cold.

Soon after I arrived, I met some folks who introduced me to a fun winter event that their friend "Watty" coordinated called GONIS. GONIS stands for a combination of GOLF and TENNIS. GO-NIS. Jim had participated in this event as a teenager with his family on the north shore of Chicago in the suburbs, and then as an adult, he kept the tradition going and brought this silly and cherished custom to the city. The group grew each year. It has been a long time since I participated in GONIS, and I am not sure they are still organizing it, but at one point we were well over thirty

When Life Gives You Lemons, Sell Them to Buy Wine!

people, which was crazy. (But awesome!)

Basically, it was something fun to do to get you through the long, dark, boring days of winter in the Windy City. Someone would get a keg and put it on a red wagon. Later, this became a garbage can with wheels so we could pull it around a bit more discreetly…just a tiny bit, mind you! The participants would each bring two or three golf clubs and several tennis balls with their name or initials or a nickname written on them. The organizers would pick a different neighborhood every year. Once it was Bucktown. Once it was Ravenswood. Once we started on Lower Wacker Drive, and once it was the West Loop. Basically, it was a pub crawl. Everyone would meet at the first bar for drinks and appetizers and then a lead person, randomly selected, would pick the first target.

Typically, the "Hole" was a fire hydrant, or a STOP sign or a garbage can far away. Some holes were par threes and others were par tens. Basically, everyone would hit their tennis ball and count how many strokes it took you to hit the target. (Back up tennis balls were needed in case one went down a sewer or into the Chicago River.) Whoever had the fewest strokes won that hole and picked the next target.

Most of us bought a driver, a wedge, and a 7 iron. The bars were organized and contacted in advance, so they knew we were coming. Some folks showed up at the first bar in a limo and had one picking them up at the last stop. I met my friend Stephen Keeney playing GONIS, and I remember he said that he had met more great people in his first six months in Chicago and had a bigger circle of friends than the three and a half years he lived

And Then...

in LA.

Every year, someone would call the police on us. Perhaps someone would look out their window and assume we were hoodlums or something. But anytime I spoke with the cops, they were laughing and seemed in awe, asking if they could join us when they got off their shift.

Stephen remembers that one year the cops did pick someone from GONIS up in the paddy wagon but brought them back to the fun a half an hour later. They probably realized, if this is their biggest problem of the day, they were getting off easily. The guy who dropped him back off said, "This is brilliant. Winters can certainly be dull, but your group is a rare find. Enjoy! I wish I thought of this! By the way, is there room for one more?"

And then...it was very clear not only to me, but all the folks participating in GONIS, that you must make the best of each situation! Winter Schminter...we had GONIS!

I first met my friend Jolene at the American Society of Association Executives annual convention trade show in Washington DC. It was probably around 2009. At this trade show, Jolene and I were getting to know each other, and she shared a story with me that I will never forget. I called my mom later that night and told her the story, and she said something she had never said to me before or since, "I want you to be friends with her!" I replied, "Mom, I am already on it!"

When Life Gives You Lemons, Sell Them to Buy Wine!

Jolene grew up on a farm outside Minneapolis, in Green Isle, Minnesota, population of 368 people. She thinks nothing of telling you how she would make squirrel stew as a kid. When she was about twenty-three, she followed one of her older brothers to Stillwater, Oklahoma, for a job with Aramark, in their management program. Her brother, John, also worked for Aramark. Jolene became great friends with her next-door neighbors, who had two little girls that she adored and would often babysit so the parents could have a date night.

One night, while the girls were sleeping over, the doorbell rang around midnight. A policeman and a priest were together on the other side of her front door with bad news. A drunk driver had a head-on collision with the girls' parents, and they were both killed. Heartbroken, Jolene made the decision not to wake them that night and figured she would tell them what happened at breakfast the next day.

The next morning, after she shared the incredibly painful news to these little girls, they were petrified wondering what would happen to them, where would they live, and who would take care of them. Their whole lives changed in an instant. They had no living relatives and did not want to be separated or sent to a foster home. So, Jolene made the decision right then and there to adopt them. Single and only twenty-four years old, she raised these girls as her own. Think about that! What an incredible human being. Today, she is a proud grandma.

Jolene is one of the most amazing women I have ever met. Her husband George Boatright is awesome as well. They make you smile and laugh by just walking through the door. George has a

And Then...

huge grin and his greeting sounds like "Hah" with his southern accent. I have been privileged to travel with them on many occasions, and they make an annual pilgrimage to Chicago to join us in the bleachers at Wrigley for the Washington Nationals vs. Chicago Cubs game. It is always one of the most fun weekends of the year. Friends are angels following you through life.

I met a great guy named Justin from Australia while skiing in Vermont in the early 1990s. Just before meeting Justin, I had attended the MPI annual convention in San Antonio, Texas and met John Potterton, the President of the Chicago Chapter of MPI at the time. Both of us are New Yorkers by birth, and we ended up singing at the piano bar called Durty Nelly's Irish Pub, on the River Walk.

I had heard many great things about Dolores, John's wife. I could not wait to connect in person. While Justin was visiting me in Chicago, we made a date for dinner at the Knickerbocker Hotel. Justin and I arrived first and then John walked in with his beautiful blonde wife in a bright red dress. I remember being awestruck right away. A new friendship was immediately formed. Later in the evening, Dolores shared with Justin that she really did not like her name. He told Dolores her name meant compassion. You can enter other peoples' sorrow with compassion. No wonder that all these years later, Dolores is a spiritual advisor.

Dolores is amazing, and several years after we met, I remember her telling me that she was once told she was wearing her claddagh ring wrong because it was facing out. Since she was married with three children, the heart should face her heart, because she was taken. Her reply was priceless. "No," she said, "this is the way I want it, as my heart is open to the world." Think about that.

Later, Dolores was diagnosed with Multiple Sclerosis or MS. A shock for her, her family, and all her loving friends. Not one to feel sorry for herself or sit around, she immediately started coordinating fundraisers for MS research and to date has raised close to a million dollars for this important cause.

Dolores decided early on that MS would not define her, and she would do everything in her power to make life better for everyone struggling with this disease.

Dolores also founded an organization called U4Uganda, a non-profit organization that lifts the children of Alenga, Uganda. She shared with me that the voice of God spoke to her since she was a child telling her to go to Africa and help children. In 2011, she visited the town of Alenga for the first time. They had no clean water and very little food. The children were sitting in the dirt to learn. That is when the idea of building them desks began. Talk about making the most of each day and helping others! She said she knew if they could get them out of the dirt, they could make everything change, and she did. They used wood from the region and hired local people in the workshop to build the desks. Within two years, they were able to furnish eight schools with desks. She returned four years after her first visit and 100 percent of the children were enrolled, test grades improved, and most of these children were moving on to secondary school. She changed their village; she changed their dreams; she changed their possibilities and inspired a generation.

And Then… I learned that her favorite quote is:

> "Service to others
> is the rent we pay for our room here
> on earth." - Muhammad Ali

Attitude is everything. Every day, we have things that could take us down if we let them. Are you going through anything now that you might need help to change?

There is always another way to look at things. Shift your perspective. Look at things from higher, lower, or even sideways. Ask a friend or family member for a different point of view; reach out to others… It can change your life for the better.

Be a Connector

My dad, Chuck McCartney, was the greatest connector ever!

Chapter Sixteen

Be a Connector

From 2003 to 2005, before I moved back to NY to be with dad while he was battling cancer, I worked for a global DMC company as VP of Sales. A colleague named Laurel Rhoads McCarthy, originally from upstate New York, and I frequently went on sales trips to Ohio.

Laurel's husband, Joe, is also from NY and a big Mets fan, so I invited them to join me in my seats for a Mets vs. Cubs game at Wrigley Field. Laurel and I became friends quickly, and I invited her to a BBQ at my home one Saturday afternoon. She bought a college friend to the BBQ named Ann, who was visiting her in Chicago. Ann was not in my front door ten minutes chatting with me and others, before she said to me, "You are a Connector!" I asked what she meant by that. She asked me if I had ever read Malcolm Gladwell's book *The Tipping Point*. I said that although I had heard him speak live in NYC, and thought he was great, I had not read the book. She said there is a section on different types of salespeople and that I was a *Connector*. Soon after, I purchased the book and read what he had to share on that topic.

He says in the book that the definition of a Connector is someone "with an extraordinary knack of making friends and acquain-

Be a Connector

tances." Gladwell says that Connectors are constantly referring people to the right expert or service to solve their problems. He shares that Connectors love networking and talking with people, just for the sake of doing it.

He says that Connector's stories always focus on the people, not the ideas or sizzle. Connectors make change happen through people. They are natural hubs. That is just the way they are oriented to the world. These are the people who every time you ask a question, they start flipping through their rolodex in the back of their mind saying, "Who do I know who knows this? Who do I know who has done this? Who do I know that I need to connect you with?" Connectors love connecting you with people because they're all about the people!"

And Then... I was just trying to be like my dad. Though he sold coal, he could have sold ice to the Eskimos. He had so much charisma and bought joy to every room he entered. People always loved being with my dad. He was my connection to the world.

Thinking how you can help others is a healthy way to go through life. It's when you give that you truly receive. The circle of life is a great thing. Think about a connection you can make to help someone personally or professionally.

Chapter Seventeen

A Lid for Every Pot

At forty-six, I had sort of given up on getting married... *and then, I met my husband.*

It is not always easy to find a person you like being around as much as they like being around you. That is really the key. I had no intentions of getting married young. I wanted to see the world, and I did. I always just figured I would meet the right guy for me around thirty-five, get married, have a few children, and continue doing my sales job and traveling. Funny how things do not turn out as you imagined. What do they say? We make plans and God laughs!

I remember when singing the national anthem at Wrigley Field on my thirty-fifth birthday, halfway through the song, I was thinking, *I forgot to get married and have kids!*

Late in my thirties, many friends were getting married and starting families. I thought something was wrong with me that I just could not seem to meet the right guy for me. I asked a friend who got help from a professional when she went through her divorce, and it made a difference. I figured it could not hurt. This was in the late 1990s. The person she recommended was a woman named Dr. Green. I called to make an appointment. Her office

A Lid for Every Pot

was a short walk from my office downtown at the time, so it was convenient. She was very nice and a good listener. It seemed important to speak to someone who did not know me already. I think I met with her maybe a total of five or six times and paid her by personal check. Though I was confident that my job would have certainly covered this expense, for whatever reason, I was afraid that someone from work might find out and it would reflect poorly on me. Now, I think that is so silly, because anyone who needs to talk through something that is upsetting them should always seek help. Life takes all of us through some hairpin turns. Finding someone to help you navigate the road does not make you weird; it makes you human! Dr. Green eventually said to me, "You seem to have amazing relationships with *all* the men in your life, but you keep yourself so busy, you don't have time for a dedicated relationship." Lightbulb! I knew she was right.

I did not want to get married to get married. I wanted to marry someone who would be my best friend and confidant. I wanted a special partner to share life's ups and downs with, someone to go to ballgames with, who was a good kisser and listener. Like most things in life, timing is everything.

Most every girl may dream of her father walking her down the aisle, but my dad died in 2005 and I did not get married until 2012. Dad died on my parents' fifty-fourth wedding anniversary, and though he lived to be eighty (not expected after his war wounds), he is still missed every day. The day after his funeral, for my forty-fifth birthday, my cousin Meg took my sister, Mom, Aunt Sibby, and me to the New York Athletic club for dinner. I remember that the background music was all my dad's favorite tunes by Frank Sinatra, Tommy Dorsey, Glenn Miller, etc. I put my

And Then...

head in my hands and began to weep. Up until then, I seemed to be holding it together as we were still running errands for Dad like selecting music for the Mass, getting the pamphlet printed for the funeral or ordering flowers, etc., all sorts of details. I had no time to mourn. My gracious cousin went up to the maître d' and tipped him generously to change the music or turn it down or off. I do not remember exactly; I just remember being sad and then grateful. After the funeral, I remember talking to my father in my head and saying, "If you see any guys you think would be a good fit for me from that high view, please send them my way."

I lived with Mom in Pelham for a year. She and my sister and I went out to dinner with our friends John and Kathy Hanson often. Their company helped get us through the pain of missing our wonderful father/husband/friend. I returned to Chicago the next year and had still not given up the hope of meeting the right guy.

On Sunday, May 4, 2008, after Mass at Old St. Patrick's Church, I walked over to some of the shops by Wrigley Field to buy baby outfits for some friends who had just given birth.

Also, my awesome cousin Teddy Weihman and his wife Sarah were expecting their first child the next week. I figured I would get them a Cubs bib, since we did not know the gender in advance.

While by the ballpark, I was chatting on the phone with my friend Margaret, who told me I had to go to Yak-zie's. She had left her raincoat there. A bartender named Brian had found it. MOD, as we affectionately call her, was in on my season tickets that year.

A Lid for Every Pot

Brian, the thoughtful bartender, while trying to figure out who owned the coat, saw that she had four tickets to about eight games in her raincoat pocket, along with a printed email exchange between the two of us. Many people would have just tried to keep the tickets, but he saw her phone number on the paperwork and called to make sure she got her coat back. (FYI, season tickets are marked and if someone tried to steal the tickets, the owner of the tickets would let the Cubs know and they would be confiscated immediately). Now, everything is done electronically, so we do not even get printed tickets unless we want to pay an extra fee.

Since Margaret told me to go there and meet Brian, that is where I decided to check on the Cubs score. I was wearing a black dress with blue flowers on it that I have to this day. I walked through the door just as the Cubs vs. Cardinals game was starting in St. Louis and asked the bartender if he knew who Brian was. He said, "I am Brian, what can I do for you?" I said that my friend Margaret had suggested I pop in and thank him again for his kindness. He said, "Have a seat, what can I get you?" I ordered something to drink and looked to my left. There was a handsome guy wearing a beige Cubs sweater. I looked down at his shoes. They were blue patent leather with the Cubs' logo all over them. I said, "I like your shoes!" He replied, "Thanks, but be careful, they are patent leather and reflect up!" In that moment, I thought, *Pay attention, this guy is cute and funny*. My mental list of what I was hoping to find was something like: cute, fun, funny, kind, likes to travel, loves me and my family, likes to party, likes sports. As time goes on, of course, your list can shrink to: he has a job *and* teeth! (Kidding, sort of!)

And Then...

While watching the game, we ended up ordering food. I shared that I had been to the Super Bowl that February, which probably impressed him more than anything else I could have said. Afterward, Gary gave me a ride home. I knew right away that I really liked this guy because he was comfortable and easy to talk to. *Comfortable* and *easy* are two words that I think are often overlooked in a relationship. I turned, smiled, and waved goodbye. He waved back.

A few weeks later, I asked him what he was thinking the night that we met when he dropped me off. He said that although I had told him to let me out at the corner that he should have dropped me at the front door anyway. Then he asked, "What were you thinking?" I honestly replied, "I hoped my ass didn't look too fat in that dress." His friend Mickey loved that story and made me tell it all the time.

The first time he stayed over, I made him pancakes for breakfast. (Heating up soup is about the best of my kitchen abilities.) I had not made them in ages and who even knows if the mix was expired, but I tried and put some blueberries in as well. He could not believe I could make rectangular pancakes in a round pan. I asked him how the pancakes were, and he replied, "Pretty safe to say you are not opening up a diner anytime soon!" I liked him even more because he was funny and honest.

A few months after meeting Gary, to make sure we were both on the same page, I asked "How do you think things are going?" He said, "I think this is the best relationship I ever had, and I love you." I said, "I love you, too!" We were off to the races. A few months later, I checked in again. He said, "Well, you like to do about ten things in a day and I like to do one or two." He had to try to pick things up, and I had to try to slow things down. A challenge for both of us, but it worked.

We dated for two years and then he moved into my place. I did not want to tell Mom because I figured she would not approve of those living arrangements. Easter weekend of 2010, Mom and Mary flew in for the weekend. Gary (though not Catholic) went to Mass with us. He had tickets to the Chicago Blackhawks game that afternoon, so I went back to my brothers in Uptown where my mom and sister were staying. I had asked my sister *not* to tell Mom that Gary was going to be moving in with me in a few months. Suddenly, while holding a cup of coffee, Mary says to Mom at the kitchen table, "Remember, I told you that Gary is moving in with Margie?" I almost dropped my coffee mug I was so shocked and upset, but later she explained that she did not want to have to keep that charade up on the East Coast. Mom turned and said to me, "I don't approve, and your father would not approve, but at the same time, I know your dad would have loved Gary because he is so down to earth, so if he is moving in with you, make sure you clear out enough space for him to feel comfortable, so he knows it's his home too." I thought, *WHO ARE YOU AND WHAT HAVE YOU DONE WITH MY MOTHER?*

We lived together for two years and got engaged on Christmas day at my brother's house. Gary had a previous commitment helping a charity but arrived at my brother's house soon after we started opening presents. A bit later, he asked me to go into the dining room to ask me something. Gary was crying when he handed me a card to read while he opened the ring box (which I did not see). I thought maybe he had cancer and I was scared.

And Then...

He had a little yellow sticky note on the card that I pulled off and it said, "Will you marry me?" And I looked up and he very emotionally said, "Will you marry me?" I said, "Yes." We hugged. I walked into the next room with the engagement ring on my finger and showed my mom first. "Guess what Gary just gave me for Christmas?" She thought it was so classy that he did that with my whole family in the next room, knowing how important they all are to me. A few minutes later in the kitchen, my adored sister-in-law Barbara Haderlein McCartney told me, "This morning, when we woke up, your brother Drew said, 'I bet Margie and Gary get engaged today.'"

During the day, I called and texted a few friends but kept pressing the b instead of the g, so my buddies were trying to figure out what "enbabed" meant.

Because Gary had been married before, we could not get married in a Catholic Church, but I was happy with the wonderful plans we set in motion. My friends Sallie and John Colucci in Pelham graciously offered to let us have the wedding in their backyard, which was our old backyard on Bon Mar Road. Naturally, we were thrilled, and it was spectacular! (Though I appreciate it was a lot of work for them!) We hired Depot Dave from Pelham, who prepared salmon and beef, and we also had a table with sushi and another with lavish charcuterie. Delicious!

Between the first and second reading, we all recited the prayer of "Our Father," which meant a lot to me. My sister Mary and nieces Madeleine and Lauren were the bridal party, plus my nephew Evan was the ring bearer and his older brother Liam helped with the pamphlets and seating. Gary's son Jon was the best man, and my oldest nephews Charlie and Sam gave me away. Unbeknownst to me, my wedding planner/neighbor/friend, Marlene Leone, had set up a plan for the part where they ask, "Who gives this woman away?" It was not covered at the rehearsal, so on the wedding day when the Justice of the Peace said, "Who gives this woman away?" I remember thinking OMG, we did not practice this part, no one will know what to say. But just as fast, my nephew Sam said, "Her mother Joan," and my nephew Charlie, dressed in his marine blue uniform said, "Her father Charles," and together they said, "And we do!" I was a puddle from there on in. Although very emotional, it was beautiful and everything I wanted. We sent a dozen blue and white (PMHS colors) balloons to heaven to my father. Several got stuck in the Dogwood tree that used to be home plate when we were kids. My oldest brother John yelled, "He knows it's happy hour. He's not leaving!" Everyone burst out laughing.

The harpist played "Take Me Out to the Ballgame" as we came back down the aisle after the service. It was perfect. We had two honeymoons. We drove up to Cooperstown to the Baseball Hall of Fame, which was brilliant. We stayed at the Otesaga Resort. Our wonderful, lavish, two-night stay was a generous gift from Gary's boss and buddy, Brian Hayford.

The second honeymoon was coordinated by my pal Jolene Boatright, who, along with her husband George, gave us three complimentary nights at the Paradises La Perla Resort in Playa Del Carmen, Mexico. We added another four nights for a full week, and it was fabulous! The room/suite was bigger than our apartment and overlooked the water. Plus, we had a hot tub on our balcony. They even put rose petals in the bathtub and had champagne on ice waiting for us upon arrival. It was magic.

We flew to Mexico for this honeymoon the day after Super Bowl Sunday the following February. It was awesome that we won $2000 in pool squares on Super Bowl Sunday. We are very lucky that way for sure! We consider Super Bowl Sunday the first big holiday of the year! Though we mostly get involved in pool squares, not large Vegas wagers, we have been lucky over the years. Do you know *anyone* who has ever won the 50–50 raffle at a sporting event? Gary has won three times at Wrigley Field. So lucky!

Gary is a good guy, handsome and funny, and though he can complain like a five-year-old, (which can be exhausting!), he has a big heart, he's a great cook and a hard worker, and we have a shared love of sports and animals, people, fun, and travel. I am proud that he worked for the same company, S & C Electric, for forty-one years and probably took five to ten sick days off total in all those years. He was very dedicated to his company, and they were great to him as well.

We had two kitties that we adored named Jackie Robinson and Addison "Addi" Sheffield (both are in heaven now). When we found our first kitty, a year after we met, Gary was not very interested and said he grew up with dogs and did not like cats. He thought it did not make sense to have a pet because I travel so much. In a matter of weeks, he became the cat whisperer and has remained so to this day!

Not every day of marriage is going to be rainbows and unicorns. However, it is wonderful to have a companion to share things

A Lid for Every Pot

with. A friend asked me once how happily married I was. I said 80 percent happy. He said I should be proud of that percentage. I have always considered myself a happy person... But remember that happiness is a moving target.

And Then... Chance encounters can help you in one way or another.

Chance meetings can change your life.

Keep looking for what you want out of life and go for it.

You never know where or with whom you will find happiness. Be open to everything, everywhere. You can find true love in a TSA line! It happened to my brother at the Charlotte airport!

From left to right are Salvatore's adorable daughthers on his lap, Lucrezia, Becky and Violante at their home in Rome.

My family on my wedding day.

Making Friends Abroad

When Mom and I knew we were meeting the Pope at the Vatican, I asked the Chicago Cubs to make this jersey as a gift.

Chapter Eighteen

Making Friends Abroad

I first met Salvatore in Florence, Italy in April 2015. Mom and I were over visiting my niece Maddy, who was going to grad school at the Johns Hopkins SEIS program in Bologna, Italy. My old company's international offices had recently closed, but our Italian saleswoman, Heather, who ran our office in Rome, was renting office space from Salvatore and connected us in case Mom and I needed something on the trip. Heather was kind enough to pick us up at the train station when we arrived in Florence from Milan and dropped us off at The Plaza Hotel Lucchesi.

The year before, I was in Italy with a group of friends renting a villa in Umbria. Prior to heading to the villa, Heather and her husband invited my husband Gary and me to their beautiful home for beverages and appetizers and then took us out to a great steak dinner at a mountainside restaurant. It is called Osteria del Milione. As it was explained to me, the man who bought the land did not want anyone else to buy the land in front of him and block the view of Florence. He asked all his friends that could afford it to chip in a million dollars each and help him buy the land. He would eventually pay them back with the money he would make at his amazing restaurant, which he did. Italians are such warm and generous people.

Mom and I planned to meet up with Salvatore in the lobby of the Plaza Hotel Lucchesi one night at 5:00 p.m. When we stepped out the door of the elevator, little did I know my life was about to change forever. I saw this handsome, clean-shaven Italian man smiling at me and Mom, and he jumped up and greeted us with "Buongiorno!" and a kiss on both sides of our face. We were smitten immediately. We went up to the rooftop bar with gorgeous views of Florence, for a glass of wine before dinner. We sat overlooking the Cathedral of Santa Maria del Fiore, and it was beautiful. Then he took us out to a feast at Trattoria 13 Gobbi restaurant where he knew everyone, and we laughed until we cried. My mom and I both fell in love with him instantly! We finally had to say that we could not eat or drink anymore. He seemed disappointed, but there would be many more nights together. On our next trip to visit him, he asked me what kind of wine my mom and I liked and when I said, "Pinot Grigio," he said, "Yuck, Pinot Grigio has no flavor." I said, "Why did you ask me then? That is what we both like to drink!" He is a hearty red wine drinker, as are most Italians!

My niece Maddy was meeting up with us in Florence for a day before we headed to see her at school in Bologna. Bologna was not on my bucket list, but I am so glad we went and spent two days and nights there visiting her. When Mom and I checked into our hotel, the front desk manager told us that our new friend Salvatore Bossone had called to get us upgraded to a suite. The friendship was doubly sealed right there.

Two years later, my mom and I returned to Italy. We took that

And Then...

opportunity to visit other friends in Europe. Our friends the Coluccis from Pelham were living in London at the time. My sister Mary flew over to London with Mom. I left a few days earlier and took my niece, Lauren, on her first visit to Ireland. She had always wanted to go. We spent two days and nights with my dear friends Conor McAuliffe and his wife Liz Heffernan in Dublin. We toured Dublin and attended a Noel Coward play at the Gate Theater. The following day we wandered through Herbert Park, met new friends, and kicked around a soccer ball. Dublin is such a great city, made better by friends who always go out of their way to show you a good time.

Then we returned to London. We got to see a great Lady Diana Fashion exhibit at Kensington Palace on April 18, 2017. Diana was a beautiful person and such a fashion icon; she was featured on more magazine covers than we can remember! After one of our many delicious dinners around town, we walked to Paul McCartney's Street and took a McCartney family photo in front of Sir Paul McCartney's house.

Several days later, Mom and I headed south over the snow-capped Italian Alps to Sicily. Neither of us had been and we were super excited. One of my favorite client/friends, Kara Ottom from Milwaukee, WI, had told me that if she ever got married, she wanted to have the wedding at the Villa Carlotta in Taormina, Sicily. As a meeting planner, she had done an event there years ago and loved it. Since I had never been, I thought what the heck and booked us into the Villa Carlotta hotel in a big suite with great windows. It was magnificent and we ended up hiring a terrific local guide and driver named Angelo, and to this day, we are friends on Facebook. We hit all the hot spots and had lunch at a wonderful seafood restaurant called l'incontro, where he knew the owner, Tony, and the service and food were outstanding! It was by far the best seafood salad I have ever had in my life. If you find yourself in Taormina, Sicily, hire Angelo and go to l'incontro to get yourself some amazing seafood salad. You will not regret it!

And Then... we flew to Rome to Meet the POPE!

Salvatore Bossone is an amazing human being. He is like a younger brother to me and set up this special day for us. My mom goes to Mass every day, so having the opportunity to meet the Pope face to face, to be able to speak with him, shake his hand, and have him bless the rosaries she bought for her friends, was a dream come true for her! Pope Frances is my favorite Pope, so I was super excited as well. Salvatore met us at the airport and drove us to his home. He and his beautiful wife, Valentina, had just had a new baby. They were so gracious and lovely and gave up their bedroom for me and Mom since it had a bathroom in suite. We connected with our old neighbor from Pelham, Nikki Striano. We had so many wonderful meals I lost count. Salvatore set us up on tours to the Spanish Steps, to the Pantheon, Trevi Fountain, the Roman Forum and Piazza Novona. All our drivers were wonderful, and most were named Marco. The black SUVs were in mint condition. It was the trip of a lifetime.

My best friend from camp, Mooie, flew over to Rome! We stayed at Salvatore's apartment downtown for two nights and did

And Then...

some exploring on our own. We took a train to Naples, and Salvatore had a car service pick us up and take us to an apartment in Positano that I found online, overlooking the Amalfi Coast. Spectacular does not even begin to describe the views we had. Breathtaking!

I had a Positano restaurant recommendation from my Chicago podiatrist, Dr. Mark Neamand, (a.k.a. The Foot Whisperer) and his Italian wife. They have visited Positano many times and know it well. Dr. Neamand is a great surgeon as well as being charming and handsome. He is happily married with three daughters, and when they go to Positano they like to visit a special restaurant at the top of the hill called Ristorante da Constantino. He even shared that if we could not get a ride there, they would come pick us up. His recommended restaurant was literally about fifty feet from the door of the apartment I had rented. Mind you, we had to walk another eighty-five steps from street level up to our apartment and balcony, but it was worth it for the amazing views. Mooie and I went to Costantino's several times; we loved it so much. We were a little later getting there on our last night, and it was already dark.

I saw a couple at a table by the window taking photos with the glorious background. Even though it was now dark, the lights lit up the sea. I said to Mooie, "I bet they are Americans on their honeymoon." She said, "How do you know?" I replied that I just did.

We sat down and started chatting with Lauren and Mike. They were, in fact, on their honeymoon. When I asked where she lived, Lauren said that they were from Chicago. I enthusiastically replied that I was also from Chicago. But then she said that she

Making Friends Abroad

had just landed her dream job and now lived in Lawrenceville, New Jersey! Mooie and I burst out laughing, and Mooie replied, "Well I live in Lawrenceville, New Jersey!" What are the chances of that conversation happening in the US, much less on the top of Positano in the Amalfi Coast?

Initially, I met my Australian friend John Price in front of the Knickerbocker Hotel around 1991. His wife Glenda (at the time) worked in a Spinal Care Unit at the Princess Alexandra Hospital in Brisbane, Australia, and she won a Winston Churchill Fellowship to travel the world and visit different hospitals to glean their information on spinal unit care and bring it back to her hometown hospital. Her husband John took a year's leave of absence to join her. That night in Chicago, the doorman at the Knickerbocker Hotel was helping me hail a cab. I saw a blonde man (John) pushing another guy in a wheelchair out of my hotel, and I asked Taha to get them a cab first. As John and his friend were getting in the car, he turned to me and said, "Do you know any fun places to go out on a Friday night in this city?" I have always felt like an ambassador for my hotel, as well as Chicago, so I said, "Well, why don't you join me and my friends? I'm on my way to meet them now!" He said, "Hop in."

A few years later, he and Glenda had a daughter and asked me to be her Godmother. They even waited until I had enough frequent flier miles to baptize her in Brisbane. Several years later, Susan and I would return for the 2000 Sydney Olympics and visited them first in Brisbane. Taryn was not yet five and couldn't pronounce "Olympics." She said, "Auntie Margie, are you going to the Bulimpics?" It was adorable.

And Then... I was reminded that the best thing to bring home from any trip is memories and new friends.

Have you met someone on a vacation who has added to the quality of your life? When was the last time you spoke with them? How about now? Might as well plan that next trip!

Susan and I visiting Glenda and John Price and my God daughter Taryn and dog Coco in Brisbane in 2000 before the Sydney Olympics.

Wanna Get Away?

*Addi (white with gray) and her mother, Jackie.
Our beloved kitties who are both in heaven now.*

Chapter Nineteen

Wanna Get Away?

Southwest Airlines commercial…

I am sure you all remember the great Southwest Airlines marketing campaign, which highlights something embarrassing like the groundskeepers spelling "Chefs" instead of "Chiefs" in the Kansas City end zone, or the general who is forced to give his password in an emergency, and it is "Ihatemyjob1." Well, one night in early June 2011, we had one of those moments.

The Chicago Bulls were in the playoffs against the Miami Heat, and Gary was going out to watch the game with his friends. I threw my back out that day, so I decided to stay home.

Gary and I had adopted two cats from the Anti Cruelty Society in 2010. We named the tiny black mother cat Jackie Robinson Phillips, and the gray kitten Addison Sheffield, dubbed Addi. As huge Cubs and baseball fans, this made sense! Addi grew up into a very big cat, and I often joked that Jackie had a fling with a mountain lion.

Addi loved to go under the radiators below our full windows that go from ceiling to above my knee. I had never even noticed the space before, but as a kitten, she would go play under there chas-

Wanna Get Away?

ing balls or fake mice. Little did I know there was a metal bar that ran the distance under there and she was growing so fast that at first it was no problem to go in and play around and get out. But as she got bigger, apparently this was a bigger challenge. Sort of like buying jeans in the size you wore the year before and realizing they no longer fit!

That night, I saw her stretched out under the radiator meowing. At first, I did not realize that she was stuck. I was watching my movie and the Bulls game and then it occurred to me she had been in the same spot meowing for quite some time. I called the front desk and one of the building's maintenance guys, Jackie, answered the phone. Jackie has worked in Lake Park Plaza for years, and I figured he might know if this had happened before. He said that I should wait an hour and if she did not get out that he would come up and see what he could do. I tried putting treats out to lure her, but her mother, Jackie, just swooped in and ate them.

This is probably a good time to tell you that since I have always traveled regularly for my job, I would often call and ask Gary to put the phone to the cats' ears so that I could say hello to them from the road. More on that later.

During that next hour, I accidentally texted my client and friend, Gary Pearson, listed on my phone as Gary P. My husband is also Gary P. In my panic, I sent the text: "Get home right away, Addi stuck in the radiator!" to the wrong Gary P. My friend quickly replied, "WRONG GARY."

I decided to call my Gary, who was not home. He said there was

And Then...

no way we could go to bed that night without getting Addi out of that radiator. After the hour was up, and nothing seemed to be working, Jackie from maintenance came up to assess the situation. At first, he thought they would have to pull out all the white paneling to get Addi out. When I asked how much that would cost to fix, he guessed it would be about $1000. We were about to do a big birthday trip with friends and family to Napa Valley, California, and had been saving up for that. We did not want to spend it that way but knew we would do whatever needed to be done. I called Gary back and told him I was giving the phone to Jackie. They spoke briefly and Jackie, the maintenance man, gave me a funny look when he handed my phone back to me.

Finally, Jackie thought he could bang the top part of the radiator wall up, the length of the room, and we could reach in and get the cat out that way. He whacked at it, and just as I reached in and got the kitty, Gary walked through the front door. We all cried; we were so happy and grateful. We tipped Jackie and snuggled with our kitty. Enough drama.

The next morning at breakfast, I said to Gary, "You won't believe what I did last night. I feel like such a jerk!" He asked, "What?" I shared that I had accidentally texted my friend Gary, instead of him, on my phone to get home right away because the cat was stuck in the radiator.

He said, "You think that's bad. When you said, 'Talk to Jackie,' I thought you were putting the phone up to the cat Jackie's ear, not Jackie the Maintenance Guy. I said to him 'MEOW, Daddy will be home soon and will give you some treats!'" I did sort of remember Jackie's eyes popping out for a moment, but I hadn't

217

Wanna Get Away?

had any idea what Gary was saying on the other end of the line.

To this day, when my friends come to the building and see our friendly maintenance man with the name Jackie on his shirt, they smile and say, "MEOW!" We thought about sending it into Southwest Airlines for their something embarrassing "Wanna Get Away?" ad campaign but figured the story would take too long to tell in a fast commercial.

And Then... Communication can be tricky sometimes but even mistakes can make you laugh in the end.

We often misconstrue what someone meant, so it's always best to recap what you heard, say it back to them, and move forward. Enjoy every moment of humor in your life. You never know when the next one is going to come your way!

Chapter Twenty

Customer Service

When my father died in 2005, my mom gave me her 1995 Black Lexus and she started driving Dad's newer car. The Lexus she gave me looked like a big mafia town car, but it was free, and I was thrilled. I was grateful to have a vehicle when I returned to Chicago.

Mom and Mary were kind enough to drive with me back to Chicago. We stopped along the way to see where United Airlines Flight 93 crashed on 9/11 in Shanksville, PA, and then to West Virginia to see the town my grandfather was born and raised in, Bruceton Mills, West Virginia. From there we headed to Michigan to visit with Si Miller and his wife Helen in Dowagiac. During the pouring rain, en route from Michigan to Chicago, we made an appointment with California Closets to set up an office for me in my guest bedroom. They came the next day. That was the first of about five times I have hired them. They are always great! That Lexus drove well for about ten years. Finally in 2016, my husband and I realized we needed to get a new car because we kept sinking money into a car that was twenty-one years old.

Since I am often in a rental car for work in a new city, I was paying attention to cars I saw on the highways across the country and narrowed it down to three to four cars I wanted to test drive. The first call was to Nissan, as I saw *so* many Nissan Altimas on the highways across the USA. Then I noticed some Maximas and thought I liked that car even better. Turns out the swirl in the door and the stitching in the console ended up being my favorite parts. They got a kick out of that!

I made a date at Mid-City Nissan dealership on Irving Park Road on the other side of I-94 to do some test drives with a salesman. Although we had many emails to confirm the appointment, he was not there at the agreed upon time. However, his colleague, Pierre Campbell, was there and went to get an Altima and a Maxima for me to test drive. Ten more minutes went by, and I told Pierre, "Your colleague and I had a date, and I have to get to work. He is not here, and I like you. If we decide to get a car with Nissan, I want to deal with *you*!"

I fell in love with the Maxima, but my husband needed to test drive it also, and I had made a date at the Audi dealership in downtown Chicago the next day to test drive an Audi A3. When I called and told Audi what we could spend, they suggested an A3. I thought, *What the heck?* I figured I would at least take a test drive. I had made a date with an Audi salesperson, and we confirmed it probably ten times. I showed up at our agreed upon appointment time and was told he was not in that day. I was furious! Zero for two with car salesmen not showing! I have been in sales my whole life and could not believe that two dealerships in a row would no show on a test drive that had been confirmed multiple times. No call, no email. Nothing! I shared my disappointment with the receptionist. A young guy in a shiny gray suit who looked like Sean Penn, a.k.a. "Spicoli" from the movie *Fast*

Times at Ridgemont High, said, "My manager would be so upset if we just let you walk out the door, so I'll give you a test drive for the A3. I figured, what could it hurt, because they were already behind the eight ball as far as I was concerned. I was pretty sold on Pierre and the Maxima.

So, the Sean Penn look-alike pulls up to me with rap music *blaring* from the car speakers of the Audi A3. I shook my head, got in the car, and turned the radio off. He probably thought, *Old fart*. We drove around a few blocks from the dealership, and I asked, "Why should I buy this car?" He looked at me and said, "Well, this is a fully loaded Audi A3." I snickered to myself, thinking, *Well that explains everything doesn't it?* I pulled up to the dealership and got out. He confidently said to me "Shall we go inside and CRUNCH SOME NUMBERS?" I looked at him and said, "Absolutely not. I am going to get the Nissan Maxima I test drove yesterday. I liked it much better and the man who took me on a test drive knew everything about the car." I walked away while his mouth was still hanging open.

Gary test drove the Maxima Friday morning at Nissan and loved it too, so we ordered one in Blue and named it Rizzo after the Cubs' first baseman. Reliable Pierre was there to meet us. They did not have a car available in blue for that weekend, so they gave us a free rental car and promised to deliver the car the next day to our condo building. Gary and I were heading to Wrigley Field for a Cubs game that Saturday afternoon, but Pierre showed up as promised that morning and spent an hour going through all the different things the car could do. Gary said, "This thing has everything but a wet bar!" I asked Pierre if he was working that day and he said yes. I did not want him to get in trouble because

Customer Service

he was spending so much time with us. He replied, "Not to worry, I told my boss you were very anal about Customer Service so it's okay!" I said, "Well, if he calls me, I can verify that and make sure he knows that they are lucky to have you on their team!" Then I posted a photo of all three of us with the car on Facebook, telling people if they needed a new car to call Pierre at Nissan.

Someone once told me that if you call an airline to book a reservation and they do not give you the customer service you deserve, to hang up and call back and maybe you will get a better rep that will be more helpful. This was great advice and it works more times than not.

In fact, it works for more than just airlines…

There is a national pharmacy near us in Chicago where we easily spend a minimum of $1,000 a year. They used to have a great guy named Ron M. who worked in their photo department, but he is gone now. Getting my Christmas cards printed has never been the same. When he first left our nearby store location, he went to another store of the same name, but it was thirty minutes farther away. Because his customer service was so good, I followed him there for a few years to do my Christmas cards. It was worth the additional hour out of my day to have someone who cared. This year, I had too much going on and his cell phone number disappeared from my cell phone for some reason. In November I had gone to the store, and they said they no longer printed cards on the premises. I know technology has made some things

And Then...

much easier, but in other ways, it has made things much harder. I pulled up the website on my phone and selected a few photos for my Christmas card. Then I wanted to change out a photo or two, but I couldn't, so I just went with what I had, just to get it over with so I could check it off my list of things I needed to do before the holidays. I was disappointed, but it was done. Gary and I were on our daily walk when I popped into the store on Irving Park Road to see if they could help me order about twenty more Christmas cards.

Upon arrival, a new, young guy in the photo department with his mask on told me to make a copy of the card, which I sat down to do. I even said that I was happy to pay more and go home and cut the cards out myself if that is what it took. It was only twenty cards, not 200! The card was an 8x3. The young guy came over and I explained what I wanted. He pointed at the screen with options and said, "These are your options." I said that none of those options were what I wanted, and I needed twenty 8x3 cards. He pointed to the screen and said, "These are your options." I thought maybe he did not understand me, and I explained again what I was hoping he could do for me. He pointed at the screen again and said, "These are your options." After he repeated that mantra about five to ten more times, I said, "Your customer service stinks!" and walked out the door. I eventually caught up to my husband walking and he said I should try their other store on Broadway when we made our lap around Wrigley Field. I did not hold out much hope, but how wrong I was.

I walked into the other store of the same name, walked to the photo department, and explained what I needed and wanted. There I met David Martinez, a store manager. This guy must have

Customer Service

taken the course in customer service because he was a gem! He could not have been nicer, and in fifteen minutes I was walking out the door with exactly what I had asked for in the first place at the first location. Walking home, I felt compelled to call the first pharmacy and ask to speak to the manager. I am 99 percent sure that the young man who loves to say, "These are your options," and *not* listen to his customers' needs or concerns answered the phone. He transferred me to a woman who had only started there a month earlier as the manager. She listened to what I had to say, apologized, and said that she would go speak to the young man and that it was not their policy to treat clients this way. I thanked her for her time and continued home. I always think that the *nicest* thing you can do for someone who has gone out of their way for you is to let their boss know what a winner they have on their team. I asked David for his boss's email, but he said I could just go online to the link on my receipt and put a note about his customer service. Minutes after I walked into my apartment, I did just that and smiled as I typed it.

I ran into David again just before I left for NY for Christmas, as I needed to pick up a prescription. I asked if he had gotten any kudos from management, and he said no. But I assured him that I had sent them a note explaining how he, as a wonderful, attentive, client-facing man, renewed my faith in customer service. He told me that I renewed his faith in people and thanked me profusely. We both had huge smiles on our faces as we turned and walked away after wishing each other a Merry Christmas.

And Then...

In the Lakeview Shopping Center on Broadway just a few blocks away from our home at Irving Park and Pine Grove, they have several things we use on a regular basis. We have a great Chase Bank, a terrific dry cleaner, and a wonderful nail salon.

Recently, Eric Guzman, an Assistant VP at Chase Bank, set up my new company. There were many confusing details and he helped me every step of the way. I was grateful and impressed with his customer service.

Fabri-care has a fabulous Korean woman named Rookie running the show, and she has dropped clothes off for me at my home when I was racing between trips. Now, that is customer service. Love her!

There is a nail salon nearby called Glamour Nails. A lovely Vietnamese woman named Quinn bought it about ten years ago and it is thriving. She is smart, hardworking, attractive, and friendly, and treats both her staff and her guests well. Quinn has done so well that she opened another location. The staff is great, and it is always packed. See what good customer service will do for you? Treat people the way you want to be treated and you will be rewarded tenfold. Glamour Nails is a total success!

Three years ago, I was in Pittsburgh meeting with customers. I took one of my favorite clients, Fran Arre, to the Pirates game while I was in town. She had invited me to stay at her home. We had met at IMEX, the biggest hospitality trade show in the USA,

Customer Service

in Las Vegas ten years ago. She told me she was from Pittsburgh. I told her I had gone to Bethany College in West Virginia (about forty-five minutes away), and she asked me if I knew her neighbors, Beth and Mark Wawrzeniak. I replied, "Know them? I was in their wedding!" We became friends in the first few moments we met.

The afternoon before the Pirates' night game, Fran and I met at the Roberto Clemente Museum. I had heard so many great things about the museum and am so glad that I went. Part of me was hoping we could host an event there the following January. Though a lifelong die-hard Cubs fan, Roberto Clemente is my husband's favorite player and my Bethany friend Evelyn's too. Evelyn is an incredible woman who grew up in the Bronx. Her father was a hero to many and unfortunately died when Evelyn was just two years old. I'm so grateful that she ended up at Bethany as a Zeta sorority sister, as she has brought so much joy into so many lives. Like my dad was to me, her dad was her hero and there is no denying Roberto Clemente was also. He was a soldier, a husband, a father, a star on the baseball field, and a humanitarian—both men taken way too young. In a way, Evelyn is a hero to many people too. She put in her time at the TV station at Bethany, and for the past thirty years has worked in NYC and is now the Program Operations Manager at WABC. Her office is next to Michael Strahan's, or should I say, his office is next to Evelyn's! She is a rock star!

I got to the museum early and went for a walk to kill time. I came across a jewelry store called Paul Michael Design on Butler Street. I walked in and fell in love with these unique earrings that were about $125. I bought them and a few months later, they broke.

And Then...

I mailed them back and they fixed them for free, and FedEx-ed them back to me. I travel a lot and often throw my jewelry into one small bag. A few months ago, one of the same earrings I bought there broke again, this time from the base of the hook, and then I lost the silver part needed to mend it. Part of me thought I should just give up and toss them out, but I really like them. They are unique, and I always got compliments when I wore them. A few years had gone by since I had bought them, and I could not remember the name of the store to call to see what could be done. I instead reached out to the Roberto Clemente Museum to see if they could give me the name of some jewelry stores nearby so I could figure this out. They were so nice and emailed me three names of jewelry stores in the area. As soon as they mentioned Paul Michael Design, I knew that had been the place. I called to say, "Hey, I don't expect you to fix these for a second time for free, but please let me know what I owe you and if you can fix them, great. I love the earrings I bought at your store!" Recently, I got a FedEx package from them with the earrings having completely new backs that look much sturdier, and there was no charge. That stuff goes a long way with me.

Great teammates make for great customer service. There is a company called Creative Group that used to be in Buffalo Grove but is now located in Schaumburg, Illinois. Their brand tagline is: *Let's Thrive*. Creative Group designs live and virtual meetings and events, plus reward and recognition programs to increase performance and inspire "Thrivability!" Their president is a woman named Janet Traphagen. She is a real dynamo and is admired in the hospitality industry. Creative Group seems to always hire great people, have wonderful clients with healthy budgets, plan awesome events, and they are a joy to work with. Yeah, I know, makes me smile too.

For years, we were not getting much of their business but then a while back, they put their DMC business out to bid. I knew that landing this account was the single biggest thing I could try to do for my old company, PRA. Our Northern California team put together the lion's share of the proposal as an example of a local office perspective, to show them what they could expect from us.

The morning of our in-person presentation, I was ready. My friend Inge had given me a dress that I wore. She knew most of the Creative Group folks well, so I felt that would be good luck. There were about half a dozen staff members in the meeting to help them make their decision. We were in the final stretch.

Though our president at the time, Denise Dornfeld, couldn't fly in physically due to another obligation, she dialed into the conference room and reiterated how dedicated we were to this process, and this account, on behalf of our company. I had prepared my thoughts and feelings as well. I was nervous, but in a good way. I committed to giving their account my priority and shared my work ethic that had been instilled in me by my dad, and my tenacity, which had been instilled in me by my mom. Though we had operated some successful programs with them in the past, I shared some quotes from other customers who had used us consistently and were thrilled with our service. If I recall, the meeting was about two and a half hours long, and their operations team asked many astute questions that impressed us.

A few weeks went by before we got the news that we had won a large portion of their business in many of our destinations. Everyone at PRA was thrilled, but most of all, I was! My interactions with their staff have always been memorable, usually fun, but always honest. Did everything run perfectly 100 percent of the time? Of course not, but it's how you deal with each situation that sets you apart. I hope they always felt like I had their back. I know when I answered my phone and it was someone from Creative Group calling for an opportunity, it always made me smile that I might have the chance to work with them on something wonderful. When it comes to great customer service, you would be hard pressed to find a better company than Creative Group to work with!

In the early 1990s, when I worked for the NRA, I was at work on a Saturday to get things done without the phone ringing all over the office cubicles. I decided to call Chase bank because I had had several issues that were not being taken care of, and I was frustrated.

I called and got a young woman who was very attentive. I shared three major concerns I had been frustrated with. She reviewed them with me and said she would call me back in a few hours after she had done some research and taken care of them.

In just a few hours, my phone rang again, and it was her. The

Customer Service

Chase rep blew me away as she went through each item on my list one by one, and then shared what she had done to take care of my concerns. Each result was exactly the outcome I had hoped for. I asked her if I could speak to her boss to tell them how impressed I was. She asked me to hold and then shortly after, her manager got on the line. I said to the man that I had been frustrated with several issues at Chase and that this woman, with one phone call, had professionally handled all my issues. I remember saying that I was sure she would move up the corporate ladder quickly.

He laughed, which I thought was an odd response. I asked, "What's so funny?" He replied, "This is her second day, and you are my third call!"

When I worked at David Green Organization or DGO, representing many hotels around the world, a local salesman named Ryan Buck worked for the Swissotel on Wacker Drive. He came over for a presentation to our sales team and then invited us for breakfast and a tour of his hotel for the following week. Well dressed, well spoken, and handsome, it was easy to immediately like Ryan. He is also smart and knows his product inside and out. I was immediately impressed with him at the office and even more so after our awesome tour.

After brief stints in San Francisco and Miami, Ryan moved back to Chicago when he got a job with the Historic Blackstone Hotel. On a client tour, he could tell you every cool story about the

And Then...

famous people who had stayed there, from Teddy Roosevelt to the Astors, Rockefellers, and Vanderbilts. He could wow you with stories about notorious visitors like the legendary mob bosses "Lucky" Luciano and Al Capone. Ryan made everything about the Blackstone interesting. You would hang on his every word.

He asked me to be a reference for him when he and Jess and their two children decided to slow things down a bit and move to upstate Michigan. A rep for the Grand Traverse Resort reached out to me years ago, and I told her that they would be crazy not to hire Ryan, as he is the real deal. He remains one of the best hotel salespeople I have ever met! He got the job. We went to visit him a few years ago, and they are loving their life there for sure!

On Thanksgiving morning last year, I got a phone call around 8 a.m. and could not imagine who would be calling me so early. It was an international call.

Turns out, it was the owner of a rug store I had visited with two friends in September 2017 in Athens, Greece. We had been out to lunch, and I was heading back to the hotel. It was then that my friend Ken noticed a cool pillow in the window of a rug store. The nephew of the owner overheard me say to Ken that I had to use the facilities, and he popped his head out and said, "You can use the ladies' room in our store." I said, "Perfect!" We entered Loom Carpets and the course of our day changed quickly. For the next few hours, the three of us sat on a couch in the back room of their carpet store, while they poured us wine and showed us rugs. We

Customer Service

made many purchases! I loved everything I purchased that day, from rugs for our bedroom and dining room, to beautiful pillowcases, to a gorgeous unique cloth piece that I have on the back of my living room couch in Chicago. The owner, Theo, wanted to say Happy Thanksgiving and see if I needed any Christmas presents he could supply. I shared that I had lost my job due to COVID-19, so it was going to be a low-key holiday for me that year.

He could not have been nicer and asked if I would put a note on Trip Advisor sharing my great experience in his store. I shared that I would, and I said that I would do one better. I would also put them on my Facebook page and mention them in my chapter on customer service in my upcoming book. Theo owns The Loom Carpets. His nephew is named Vahan, and he was very helpful as well when we visited, showing us countless different rugs, and never complaining about pulling them out of oceans of stacks.

Having been in sales my whole life, I was so impressed that this man took the time to place an international call looking for his next sale. Theo probably went through old receipts and saw that I had spent a good deal of money at his shop. He asked that I please share his store information with whomever I could, and I have. If I ever make it back to Athens, one of my first stops will be at The Loom Carpets! What a dedicated salesman! After we left his store, he walked us to his sister's jewelry store where I purchased a pretty necklace with matching earrings that I love to wear. Discount if we paid cash. You are on!

And Then... I learned once again the value of keeping your word, knowing your product, and knowing your audience!

And Then...

It takes very little to be above average, because so many people just don't care!

Have you had a great or bad customer service experience that you will always remember?

When you are faced with service that is not average, remember, it's how you deal with each situation that sets *you* apart.

Theo Liaibis is the owner of The Loom Carpets in Athens, Greece. We bought rugs, throws, pillow cases and more. Great customer service and he even made an international call to follow up!

Customer Service

Pierre Campbell from Nissan - a customer service champion.

Chapter Twenty-One

Timing is Everything

When my friend Paul Hayward got married in 1993 in St. Michaels, Maryland, he finally connected me to a guy he thought I would be great friends with and had wanted me to meet for years. His name is Larry Altmann. They knew each other through the Bethany Soccer Alumni Association.

Larry was a stand-out soccer and lacrosse player at Bethany, but it was before I arrived there. Larry grew up in Irondequoit outside of Rochester, New York and played hockey in the Kleehammers' backyard hockey rink where the local kids in town gathered to play. He knew my friend Beaver's older brother Mike best. Larry got to know Beaver Kleehammer well when they both played attack on the Bethany Lacrosse Team.

From Chicago, I flew to Baltimore/Washington airport on Southwest for the wedding, and Paul and his fiancé, Michelle, picked me up at the airport. I had never met her before. The Thursday night festivity was a barbeque at a friend's house, and that is when Larry and I first connected. We quickly could see why Paul wanted us to meet.

Timing is Everything

Neither of us are shy and both have lots of passion for Bethany, friends, sports, and fun!

I distinctly remember one conversation with Larry. It is not one you would forget. For whatever reason, Larry started speaking in fluent German. I said, "Wow, that is impressive. How did you learn to speak German so well?" He replied that his dad fought for Germany in WWII. My beer was halfway to my lips, but I pulled it back down. I looked at him in shock and said, "No one has ever said that to me before. My dad fought against Germany and Hitler in WWII. My dad fought with Patton in the Battle of the Bulge." He said his dad was like all the other young German men in his generation; they were expected to become part of Hitler's army. That was what growing up in Germany was like in the late '30s and early '40s.

As our conversation ensued, I said, "Wouldn't it be wild if my dad and your dad were in the same town on the same day shooting at each other, and here we are just a generation later sharing a beer in Maryland?" Then I shared that my dad had marched from Nancy to Metz in Belgium. Larry looked at me and said, "My sister is named Nancy because my dad was stationed just near Nancy in Luneville." Goosebumps! Then Larry shared that his father had in fact written a book that he never published. Mr. Altmann wrote his memoir from the eyes of a German soldier. I asked Larry to send it to me so I could share it with my father. Dad and I were blown away, as Larry's dad shared many very intimate things. One story was about him being on a convoy that was stop and go. He thought

And Then...

he would have time to take a shit in the woods, but then the Americans were coming. Unfinished, he had to pull up his pants and jump back on the truck. A reminder that we are all human beings.

At one point, Mr. Altmann had shrapnel through his ankle from US howitzers miles away. He ended up on crutches. The Americans controlled the air and would strafe the trains delivering ammunition and supplies to the front lines. One night, the train Larry's dad was on stopped when they heard the American planes overhead. The German soldiers ran for the woods to hide, but since Mr. Altmann was injured, they did not bother to stop and help him off the train. It was every man for himself. The Americans strafed the train and there were casualties. Mr. Altmann survived.

My dad read the book and figured that they had missed each other in Nancy by just one week. My father said the TV show *M*A*S*H* was pretty much what it was like in make-shift hospitals where they patched him back together twice. Once when a bomb blew up near his head, it left him mostly deaf in his right ear. The other injury was being shot by a sniper who put three bullets in his stomach in January 1945 in St. Vith, Belgium. I remember him telling me as a little girl that he was shot right before his platoon, the 87th Infantry of Patton's 3rd Army, marched over the Bridge at Remagen.

Mr. Altmann ended up in a large American POW camp in Northeastern France, near Nancy in Belgium. These POW

Timing is Everything

camps were often located adjacent to Exit Depots. An American battalion would be relieved and would drop off their vehicles before being shipped home. Since he spoke decent English, he was valuable to the Americans. For the last year and a half of the war, he was organizing inventory from pots and pans to tanks and Jeeps and getting them sent back to the USA. One American soldier named Robert helped get Larry's dad into the USA. There he met his wife at the University of Rochester. They fell in love and got married, but Larry shared that his mother's father was not a fan of this union and did not go to the wedding, nor really speak to his son-in-law until he was on his death bed. There he said to his son-in-law that he had been a good husband to his daughter and a good father to his grandchildren, and then…he died.

This story has always stayed with me. Just thinking that timing is everything. One week either way, one bullet one inch over, one piece of shrapnel a foot higher, could have been the difference between our fathers living or dying, and obviously to either me or Larry never coming into this world. In the end, Mr. Altmann was this terrific man and terrific father, who was not happy that Hitler came to power in his homeland but did what he had to do to survive. I bet he and my dad would have enjoyed sharing a beer together, too.

And Then… I was reminded that many people are misunderstood for reasons beyond their control.

Have you taken the opportunity to see past a label and get to know the person inside?

And Then...

Move past a stereotype. Today particularly it's too easy to see people as labels. Take the time to get to know someone... find the common denominator.

With Mary Kay and Larry Altmann in Maryland. His dad and my dad fought against each other in the war

Dad and his grandchildren in front of Pelham Town Hall in 1999 when he was Grand Marshal.

Bastogne

Charles McCartney from Battle of the Bulge, which hangs in an 87th Infantry museum as well as a café in Bastogne, Belgium from when he was nineteen years old.

Chapter Twenty-Two

Bastogne

*This chapter is dedicated to my father
Sgt. Charles McCartney
I & R Section, 2nd Battalion
375th Infantry Regiment
87th Infantry Division, US ARMY
(1925-2005)*

*Also, to our beloved friend
John Colucci, Gunnery Sergeant, US Marine Corps (1958-2021),
who died suddenly a week after reviewing facts for this chapter
with me…*

They loved each other, and we loved them.

In March 2003, my father, three brothers, and several other relatives and friends went to tour my dad's battlefields from WWII in Belgium. They arrived via two vans from Paris to the Ardennes Forest area of the Battle of the Bulge on a chilly afternoon. They visited the site where many years ago, my dad's unit got off trucks after a long night on the road driving the long way around where the Germans had already taken ground in the shape of a huge bulge. Hence the name.

After looking over the crossroads where my dad and his comrades disembarked, they visited some woods where foxholes were still

243

visible from about fifty-eight years earlier. It was an amazing site. Though I was not there at the time, I read about the experience in my nephew's application to Princeton. Charlie had to write a tribute essay and he talked about my dad, and the moment he slumped into one of those foxholes on this trip. Foxholes that had been occupied by him on many long nights when he was just a teenage soldier. Dad cried at the sight and shared that, "Although I am not proud of what happened in these woods, it was for the greater good of mankind."

John Colucci, part of the Pelham contingency, shared with me that when the visitors got back in the vans, it was getting toward dinnertime. They went back to the hotel in Bastogne as a somber group before heading to a local restaurant for dinner.

At the dinner, in what seemed a typical Belgian restaurant, they were seated at a large table in the middle of the room. There were approximately sixty other customers in the place. While being served, the owner and his wife came out and walked up to my father. They asked him if he was a veteran of the Bulge, and he answered, "Yes." After speaking to my dad, the owner, a man in his thirties or so, asked for silence in the restaurant. Everyone quieted down, and the owner told the crowd in French that they were fortunate to have a hero in their midst who was responsible for saving their country in the war. The crowd erupted in applause and there was not a dry eye in the group. The owner introduced his children to Dad and repeated what he had told the audience. For those who think people in Europe have forgotten the sacrifice of the WWII generation, remember this story.

The tour guide my brother had hired was a great Belgian guy named

And Then...

Pascal. I must correct myself here, because "hired" is the wrong word. He would not take any money from us. He said his mother told him, "Always be good to the Americans, because if it weren't for them, we'd be speaking German." When we visited, we did take him and his wife Natalie out to dinner and we brought them gifts from New York. I invited Pascal to our wedding, as a friend and as a tribute to Dad, but unfortunately, he could not make it.

When Mom and I were on our trip, we started in Bruge in early September. We took several boat tours and enjoyed all the beautiful restaurants and flowers everywhere. We spent two nights there before we drove to Bastogne. That drive took us *way* longer than we anticipated. We thought we would arrive for a late lunch, but it was dark before we pulled into town. Many towns in Belgium have two different names, listed in French and in Flemish on road signs, which makes navigating more difficult. At one point I got to a place where I had to stop the car and show credentials, which I thought was strange. I asked the man if we were in Tourcoing or Tournai (Doornik in Flemish) and he said, "Neither, you are in France." Swell.

Pascal connected us with his friend in Manhay who owned a great Bed and Breakfast called Bo Temps. They showed us several sleeping rooms to choose from, but when we saw the sunflowers, we knew that was the one for us. Sunflowers have always been my favorite flower, because they are so happy looking and remind us of our dad. Their young sons Tom and Ben had a little museum set up in their backyard with artifacts from WWII, most of which they found in their own backyard. They took great pride in sharing this with Mom and me.

One of the signs in the area read: "After hard-fought battles outside this town in the Winter of 1944-45, the 87th Infantry division (Golden Acorn) of General Patton's army seized St. Hubert from the Nazi forces and preserved it intact for the benefit of its Belgian Citizens."

We even visited Pascal's friend Oliver's museum tribute to the Golden Acorn Division, where they first unveiled a photo of my father. Then at the end of our second day of tours, they took us to McAuliffe Square in downtown Bastogne, where they have a bust of McAuliffe and his famous reply to the Germans after they asked him to surrender: "NUTS!"

We entered Café au Carre and saw an amazing Battle of the Bulge memory wall and then, to our surprise, Pascal had orchestrated Dad's photo (at age nineteen in uniform) to be unveiled there, too. I remember Mom saying, "Your dad would be a lot prouder that his photo is hanging in this saloon than any museum!" Naturally, we were super proud of both unveilings!

From there we found an *amazing* museum dedicated in 2007 by a survivor of the Massacre of Malmedy for his murdered fellow soldiers. It is called Baugnez 44 Historical Center and it blew us away. It shows what happened on December 16 and 17, 1944. Hitler launched a massive counteroffensive in the west. A convoy of around thirty American vehicles had been advised to change its route, but it stuck to its original route. While passing through a junction, the American convoy came under fire from Peiper's men, forcing its lead vehicles to stop. Overcome by the enemy, the Americans surrendered to Peiper's SS. The Germans took their valuables and placed them in a field just south of the Baugnez crossroads. Under armed guard, they were later machine gunned in what has come to be known as the infamous "Malmedy Massacre." One soldier played dead under the bodies of his friends. Later, when the coast was clear,

And Then...

he snuck away over a hedge and lived to tell the story.

That amazing tribute had not been there when Mom and Dad came back in the 1950s or 60s, but she clearly remembered going to the Malmedy Memorial. It was important to Mom that she show it to me. It was getting dark out and starting to rain. We were heading to Brussels that night to eventually connect with my friend, Eric Rozenberg. We started down a hill and I said to Mom that I did not think we would be able to find it. Suddenly, we saw a sign. She burst into tears and begged me to turn the car around, saying how much it meant to her, and she would probably never be there again, so I did. It was just a quarter of a mile behind us! So glad I made that U-turn! They have the names of approximately eighty American soldiers on wooden plaques in the stone wall. The altar at the memorial has a huge cross and a mantel paying tribute to the Americans with photos, prayers, candles, and wreaths. *Every* single day, the locals make sure there are also fresh flowers on that mantel.

The plaque reads:

"To the memory of the soldiers of the United States Army who while prisoners of war were massacred by Nazi Troops on this spot on 17 December 1944."

Eventually, we made it to the Hilton in Brussels where their sales manager sent a chilled bottle of champagne and upgraded us to a suite with a great panoramic view of the city. Mom was in her glory, calling everyone back home to tell them about our adventures thus far.

The next day, Eric, a Belgian native whom I had met at an MPI Leadership event in Dallas, took us to an amazing, delicious lunch. When we walked into the elegant restaurant, Eric introduced us as the wife and daughter of an American hero who helped liberate Belgium. Mom and I were once again bursting with pride.

Eric had shared his own amazing story with me about his dad! At eight years old, his lovely father, whom I had the pleasure of meeting, was a Jewish child being hidden from the Nazis by the Jouan Family, who owned a farm in Thynes, near Dinant, not far from Bastogne. This child was helping move the cattle on the land when German tanks that were racing to get to the Battle of the Bulge came upon him. He had the cattle blocking the road. A German soldier put a gun to his head and said, "Make the cows move faster, or I will shoot you!" Another German soldier said, "Don't shoot him, or the cows will move slower or not at all." So, the German with the gun holstered his weapon. I cannot even imagine the fear in that little boy who did what he could to help in his own way. Thankfully, he survived and thrived and raised his own family back in his hometown of Charleroi.

One story I will always remember is how my dad shared the constellation Orion saved his life during WWII. (Thus the cover of the book!) He and another soldier from their platoon were on an intelligence mission to see where the Germans were that night. They were in a small boat on a river or a lake or pond. I don't remember where. Before they left, they looked up and saw Orion, one of the most prominent constellations that is visible throughout the world and easily recognizable in the night sky.

Hours had passed as they traveled on their boat with a compass

And Then...

and gear and eventually, they could hear the Germans' voices. They quickly headed back to camp to let their platoon know where the enemy was. Though tired and cold, they followed Orion, a hunter in Greek mythology, and headed safely back to their base.

To this day, whenever I am looking at the stars, I look for Orion to give him a wink and a smile of gratitude for being my dad's beacon of hope when he was only nineteen years old, fighting for his country in a strange land, far from home.

And Then... A community isn't always a neighborhood. Connecting with people over a shared sense of pride is very powerful. We can all feel related to people who share our beliefs and our appreciation for those who helped make our world a safer place.

Memorial Day is for us to appreciate those who made the ultimate sacrifice and did not come home.

What is your holiday or occasion to create more connection? Could you do more to foster and encourage the sense of community around you?

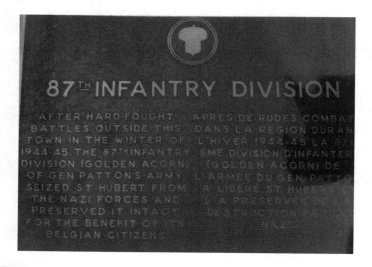

John Colucci and my Dad

The son of Bo Temps Bed & Breakfast owners, Tom, seen here. Tom and his brother, Ben set up this museum with artifacts, from the War, found in their back yard near Manhay in Belgium.

Chapter Twenty-Three

The Museum of Life

In 2016, after watching *Downton Abbey* religiously and seeing the Royal Viking River Boat Cruise sponsor ads at the start of each show, I thought… I want to do one of those cruises! Promptly, I asked my mom and sister if they might be interested in doing the Danube Cruise, which left from Nuremberg, Germany, and ended in Budapest, Hungary. They were both down, and we booked our trip. It was in June, over my birthday, and I remember they made a cake out of white towels on my bed. Then they sprinkled small hard candies in a variety of colors around the "cake" and on my bed, so it looked like little flowers. It was so nice and thoughtful and very much appreciated. The name of our ship was *Freya*. Our stops were Regensburg, Passau, Krems, Vienna, and we ended in Budapest. During the trip there were heavy rains in Paris that affected the levels of the water on the Danube. On my birthday, the boat had to remain docked, I believe in Passau. We had the choice to go on a five-hour round-trip bus ride to see a church and town or stay on the boat. I decided I would rather sit on the top deck with my sister and read and play cards and drink wine in the sun with her and Mom than sit on a bus most of the day, so that is what we did and we had a great time.

Mary and I did the pre-package trip to Prague, since we had never been there before and were interested in exploring. Prague is a wonderful city, and we had a great group. My Aussie friend John Price, while still living in Australia, met a Czech couple visiting his best friend back in Brisbane. The husband was hoping to learn English and his wife, Pavla, worked for a Destination Management Company back home in Prague.

When I was heading to Prague, John connected us with Pavla, and we got together. We ate at an amazing restaurant we never would have found on our own. That is why these contacts are great to utilize, as they know all the extra special spots! The name of the restaurant was Hotel U Prince, and we sat on the rooftop overlooking the city. The food was outstanding, and we shared a lot of laughs. We even got an awesome firework show! It is located close to the old Town Hall with an Astronomical Clock, which is also very cool.

Eventually, we took the bus to head to the start of our cruise and to connect with Mom in Nuremberg. We toured the courthouse where the Nuremberg Trials were held after WWII, and that was incredibly powerful. Hard to look at photos of young girls swooning over Hitler in the museum, though.

We loved everything about the cruise, but Mom was anxious for us to get to Vienna to see her friend Daisy, who was her bridge partner in Pelham for a very long time. Daisy was originally from Budapest, Hungary.

The morning we arrived in Vienna, Daisy came to the ship to spend time with Mom, while Mary and I went on one of the local tours. I had been to Vienna before when I went to school in

And Then...

Austria, but Mary had not. The plan was to return to the ship, go to lunch in town with Daisy and Mom, and then head out to some museums, after dropping them at Daisy's apartment, which was huge and gorgeous. She treated us to her favorite wiener schnitzel spot for lunch called Café Landtmann, where the service and food were spectacular, and she knew everyone. We walked back to her apartment, which was maybe seven blocks away. Daisy poured us each a welcomed glass of cold water on a hot afternoon. We sat down and once she began to speak...it became imminently clear to us that we were not going anywhere. We had our own live museum of words unfolding before us, right there.

Daisy shared that her family was Jewish. I never knew that her entire family had converted to Catholicism when she was a child in the 1920s, when there was a mass conversion of the Hungarian Jewish aristocracy to Christianity by way of demonstrating their loyalty to Hungary. During WWII, before Hitler's army invaded Hungary, her father, Ferenc Chorin, was a member of Parliament. One night, he and his wife hosted a big party at their house. It was the night before the Nazis invaded Hungary. Daisy was nineteen years old at the time and had an older sister and younger brother. Ferenc Chorin was also one of the most important public figures in industry at the time, head of the industrialist's organization. His wife, Daisy Weiss, was the daughter of Manfred Weiss, a Hungarian industrialist who effectively bought the heavy steel industry to that country through the Weiss Works which became the core of the Manfred Weiss Steel and Metal Works. He had more than 30,000 workers at this plant on Csepel Island, making him one of the biggest industrial employers in Europe.

The Museum of Life

One person who didn't attend the party at the Chorins' home that evening in March was Regent Horthy, who was in Germany meeting with Hitler. Daisy's family had heard the rumors about the concentration camps but couldn't imagine that this was happening. The biggest concern was that Germany would become impatient with their Hungarian ally because of its more lenient policies toward the Jews there. They feared it was just a matter of time before the Nazis attacked Hungary as well. The next morning on March 19, 1944, at 5 a.m., the phone rang at their home. A voice on the other end said, "The Nazis are coming for you now. Leave immediately!"

The son left with the nanny to a prearranged hiding place. The two daughters left with their mother to a prearranged hiding place. Their father met his brother-in-law, Moric, and the two of them went to a monastery about sixty miles away, near Lake Balaton. The phone lines were tapped, and Ferenc Chorin could not help but call as many people as possible during that calamitous time. Finally, Nazi soldiers arrived at the monastery and threated to burn it down should the two men not be released, which they were.

Chorin and Kornfeld were taken to a Gestapo jail in Budapest, interrogated, and then moved to Mauthausen, where they stayed until Kurt Becher, an adjutant of Heinrich Himmler, went and got him out. There were many interests competing for the factory, which was manufacturing Messerschmidt engines for the Germans. By this point, assets of the Jewish family members had already been nationalized. With Himmler's approval, the SS took a "Lease" for twenty-five years on the largest industrial empire in Hungary in exchange for the family's lives and imminent departure, forty members of whom were permitted to travel to Portugal and Switzerland. Daisy and her family were flown to Lisbon and while awaiting transport to America, Daisy learned to play bridge on the docks. Knowing that they might need an exit strategy, Ferenc Chorin Jr. had been sending money to NYC for some time before their family finally arrived in NYC in 1947, where he played an active role among Hungarian immigrants.

This is a story that has been told in many shapes in many forms. It is a story of survival. They were "lucky" to have the privilege of money, but they still lost a lot. Those were very dark times that we hope we never see again.

But to carry on with this amazing story, long after the war had ended, Daisy was working in NYC. She had a cousin coming over from Hungary to visit and there was some fancy-dress ball they were attending. Daisy had a date but was looking for a man to be her cousin's escort. She thought of her friend Rudy Strasser, from Austria, whom she had met before and who also lived in NYC. She was going to call him when, ironically, she bumped into him on the streets of NYC and told him about the ball. She asked if he would be her cousin's date. He replied that he did not like fancy balls but asked if *she* was free for dinner that night. And the rest, as they say, is history.

Rudy is an amazing man who was in prison in Duesseldorf and Krefel during the war for helping with the underground. Someone they thought was their friend turned them in to the Nazis. Some of his friends were executed. Rumors were rampant that the war was ending soon. Rudy and the last surviving friend he had in prison near Vienna decided to make a break for it. The

Germans were covering up their tracks, and Rudy and his friend were afraid they might all be killed. They somehow broke out of jail and rolled down a hill into a forest. They heard gunfire on the left and gunfire on the right and were not sure which way to turn. They turned left and stumbled right into a troop of American soldiers who were on their way to liberate the prisoners. The Allies were dropping food packages out of planes. The prisoners were so malnourished that they dove for the food packages all at once. Somehow, Rudy couldn't get to any of the packages, which ended up lucky for him; most of his fellow prisoners died after eating them because their systems couldn't handle all the foot at one time!

After hours of listening to Daisy's amazing stories in her living room, we took a cab back to our ship. On Facebook that night, I posted a photo of us at lunch and shared just a bit of her tale. That was a Thursday. On Friday, my friend Dawn Penfold replied on Facebook that she couldn't believe that I knew Daisy because she is her husband's favorite cousin. They were all just together for a "Descendants of Manfred Weiss" reunion in Budapest a few years prior. I was in shock. This could have gone in the small world chapter, but wait, there is more!

On Friday, we docked in Budapest and had twenty-four hours there for tours before most folks were flying home the next day. However, I had friends in Budapest, so I stayed an extra night. Five minutes after I checked into the Budapest Hilton, Thomas, my Irish friend, whom I knew through Conor from when he was a bartender at the Hague, called my room from the lobby. He was ready to be a tour guide. We wandered around town and grabbed lunch. The money and language were different there

And Then...

and it was confusing, so I was glad to have him translate. That evening, we met up with his girlfriend Adrienn Kefei, a Hungarian native. Thomas had explained to me that at the time, Budapest was bidding on hosting the Olympic games for a future year. If selected, however, they were going to have to build more hotels. The reason Adrienn could not be with us that day was because she was with two wealthy Americans from Miami who were looking to build a hotel on Csepel Island. Yes—the same island where Ferenc Chorin operated his plant! He shared that if that happened, he hoped to build, operate, or manage an Irish pub there and would hope my husband, Gary, could come over and help him bartend for the Olympics. I said, "YOU ARE ON." He said Adrienn would join us for dinner that night. We had a great time at dinner laughing and catching up and then went back to the Hilton for a nightcap. I wanted to get to bed at a decent hour, as I had an early flight back to the USA. Another cruise ship had docked in Budapest, and there was a large group of guys from the ship who were cheering, watching a rugby match, and Thomas could not resist joining in on the camaraderie. This left me and Adrienn the opportunity to catch up one on one.

So now, this was Saturday night. I started to share with Adrienn the stories Daisy had shared in Vienna about her family, the Chorins, and Weisses just two days earlier, and the connection to my friend Dawn in the USA. Her mouth dropped open. She looked at me and said, "I have chills. The reason I was not with you and Thomas today was because the location where the Americans wanted to build a hotel, possibly for the Olympics, is in an abandoned plant on Csepel Island." She pulled out her phone and showed me photos. Amazingly, there is a red rug *still* at the front door that has MW on it for, Manfred Weiss...Daisy's grandfather.

And Then... It hit me, how interconnected life really is. My mom, her bridge partner, the girlfriend of a bar manager, and a whole other cast of characters brought to life an amazing history that went full circle in just three days! Wednesday Daisy, Thursday Dawn, and Friday Adrienn.

We never know how one chance meeting will connect us with others throughout the world. What people have *you* met who have changed the course of your life?

Daisy Strasser, my sister Mary, Mom and Me in Vienna - Post wiener schnitzel lunch, before walking to Daisy's and having the amazing story unfold of her family surviving WWII.

Giving Thanks

Firstly, I'd like to thank my brothers and sister.

John's success fulfils my dad's dream of making sure that the family will always be taken care of. He is also a great dad.

Mary is the bridge for all of us and the greatest sister I could ask for.

Drew is happily married, successful, and a wonderful father.

Ray followed his dreams to become a coach, and we all admire that!

Since COVID-19 hit, our world has been turned upside down. We all know how hard the doctors, nurses, EMTs, police, firefighters, and teachers have worked. How hard the restaurant and bar owners have worked to try to stay alive, and how many wonderful establishments we have grown to love have had to close their doors. Not sure if the hospitality industry will ever bounce back to where we were before. Tough to bring people together to create great memories when we are encouraged to stay in small groups to be safe from this deadly Coronavirus that

Giving Thanks

has killed over half a million people to date in the USA alone. But this will eventually end, hopefully sooner rather than later!

I feel compelled to do a shoutout to several caregivers of our mother.

Mom's Pelham neighbor, Jim Donahoe, has been a blessing from the time they moved next door. Jim's dad, John Donahoe, went to PMHS with my mother, though he is a few years younger than Mom. Jim is a driver, a landscaper, an organizer, a fixer of everything, a cat lover and sitter, and a great friend to our mom and all of us too. Mom has often said, "If Jim ever moves, we have to move next door to wherever he goes!"

Also, my sister from another mother, Sallie Saunders Colucci, who fortunately still lives two golf shots from my mother's front door. Sallie has gone to visit my mom almost every night at 5 p.m. since the virus hit. When I was still working, HH meant Hilton Honors. Now, it means Happy Hour! Sallie sometimes brings along her awesome kids, Jake, Annie, or Grace. Mom is always so happy when they come too. We have an etagere in our front hall, and it is filled with pictures of them, so Sallie always says that when she is at my mom's, she feels like she is home anyway! This guarantees that Mom gets to see at least one other person each day!

Since the start of COVID-19, we have heard so many stories about nursing homes. Some good, some bad. Like most things in life, it is a crap shoot. However, through the grace of God or good Irish luck, we have two dedicated Irish women who have cared for my mother in her own home, in the town she was born in and loves, for over two years now. They are *amazing*. They treat our mother like she is their mother. They are kind, dedicated, fun, and nice. Mom is always happy. In addition to daily Mass, they take her walking either to the park or up and down her street. She is in great shape, and as she says every day when people tell her how wonderful she looks… "Not bad for an old lady!"

So, to Norrie Coen and Trish Eccles, a huge heartfelt THANK YOU! I could not finish this book without recognizing how much my siblings and I appreciate the wonderful care you have given to our beloved mother, Joan McCartney. Thank you for your love and dedication. She loves you and we love you for your dedication and care, and we recognize all that you have done for her to keep her happy and safe. My dad is surely looking down from heaven very proud, as the last thing we said to him in the hospital before he died was, "Don't worry, we will look after Mom," so he knew that it was okay to go.

He is probably at Heaven's Rainbow Room checking out some bands now, so when the day comes that Mom joins him, hopefully years from now, he can saunter over to the Pearly Gates and immediately whisk her onto the dancefloor. I envision Frank Sinatra playing in the background, and them holding each other tightly, where they started, where they will end, where they belong…together.

And Then…

Mom and Dad on their wedding day.

Acknowledgements

Thank you to Kerry Kathleen Heaps, a.k.a. "Coach" from Book, Speak, Repeat in Orlando for inspiring me to make this amazing journey!

To Karen Smith for your help with early editing and the website. To Joan Sheehan for your assistance with historical information about OLL Camp.

Special thanks to Donna Wolfe, Jim Grillo, Timmie Cortina and Heather Brown. Thanks to Judi Holler, Jean Antoniou and Kerry Drew Crowe and Jackie Newkirk. Thanks to Joe Doiron & Wynne Anne Meaney, Julie & Jeff Shewman, Michelle Parlier, Betsy Garcy, Shelley Wells, Nancy Chambers, Margaret & Steve Smith, Donna Grande & Mark Ward and Dana Trainor. Thanks to Dan & Dawn Vogelhuber, Anne & Perrin Stephens, Trish Striano, Tina O'Keefe Holly and Gerry Holly, Murray Ryan, Bernice McArdle, Pat & Rachel Dunn, Karen & Park Allison, All the Colucci's, Karen & Mike Brennan, Meg Barry, Jane & Harold Block and all the Weihmans. Thanks to Dan Fornier, Hillary Eaton, Melanie Marshlow, Lisa Croce, Michelle Pagnucco, Vivian Demarinis-Haik, and Resi Donovan.

Thanks to Jess Gancarski for being our cat sitter so we could take so many trips to NY to visit Mom. To the countless friends and strangers who have shown their kindness to me and those I love over the years, thank you from the bottom of my heart.

When accepting the MPICAC Hall of Fame award at Galleria Marchetti, Habtamu was right by my side along with my family (June 2, 2021).

So happy that my friends and family could join in the celebration too!

About Margie McCartney

Margie McCartney is an engaging and effective speaker who reminds her audience of the importance of being open to all experiences and translating them into personal and professional successes. Margie has over three decades as an international hospitality ambassador, connecting people from different backgrounds and building beneficial networks on three continents. Telling stories about the importance of networking and making connections, whether with an Ethiopian cab driver in Chicago or an Armenian stranger in a Moscow restaurant. Margie will entertain and educate your audience.

About Margie McCartney

In June 2021, she was awarded the Meeting Professionals International CAC Hall of Fame Award, after previously being honored as a Supplier of the Year. She has also been honored by Professional Conference Managers Association, Chicago Chapter, with the Pillar award.

McCartney is currently the Director of Global Sales for the DMC Network and President of McCartney Partners.

A Pelham, New York native, she has called Chicago home for the past 32 years. An avid Chicago Cubs fan, she lives in Wrigleyville with her husband Gary, and their two cats, Cubbie and Harry Caray.

Book Margie McCartney to Speak at Your Next Event
for these popular speech topics & more

The Kindness of Strangers

Sometimes we win the lottery of life and don't even know it. Everyone in our life started out as strangers. People come into our life for a reason, a season or a lifetime. There are lessons with each interaction so whether you are dealing with difficult people, a new family member or interacting with a stranger on the street, always look for the good in others to bring out the best in you.

Customer Service

We all know how it feels to get good service. We all know how it feels to get bad service. It can set the tone for your day or week!

Sometimes you may need to hang up and call back to get someone with a better attitude. Be the memorable person who went above and beyond. Typically, If people have a good experience they tell four people, if people have a bad experience, they tell ten people!

It's OK to be a BOZO

When life gives you lemons, sell them to buy wine. Life is a series of events and if we don't take the time to add in a little fun and humor, it makes a dull ride. This workshop will teach you how to not only laugh at yourself but being able to put other people at ease in stressful situations.

Go to: McCartneyPartners.com

CONNECT WITH MARGIE

Contact Margie McCartney

McCartneyPartners.com
McCartneyPartners@gmail.com

Connect with Margie McCartney

linkedin.com/in/MargieMcCartney
instagram.com/McCartneyMargie
twitter.com/McCartneyMargie